If it is to be, the

Farrell J Cluber

2/8/20

AFRICAN AMERICAN WARRANT OFFICERS – THEIR REMARKABLE HISTORY

Farrell J. Chiles

Published by BookLocker.com, Inc., St. Petersburg, Florida.

Printed on acid-free paper.

BookLocker.com, Inc.
2018

First Edition

Dedication

In Memory of

**Chief Warrant Officer Five (Retired) Rowmell R. Hughes
(May 7, 1948 - December 4, 2015)**

and

**Chief Warrant Officer Four (Retired) Leonard A. Dungey
August 10, 1919 – December 3, 2017**

"Quiet Professionals"®

Acknowledgements

Special thanks to all the Warrant Officers, and their families, who contributed the biographies, stories, photos, and articles to make this project successful.

African American Warrant Officers –
Their Remarkable History

Contents

Foreword

Farrell Chiles has once again made history surpassing all previous accomplishments as a decorated veteran, executive public servant, and now seasoned author of his latest book, *African American Warrant Officers - Their Remarkable History*. In this release, Mr. Chiles relies primarily on African American Warrant Officers providing information about themselves and their willingness to share their biographies, stories, photos, contributions, and achievements in the military and in their civilian life.

In 2005, Chiles was the pioneer who researched and contributed to the United States Army Warrant Officer Association's (USAWOA) Newsliner Newsletter. His writings included contributions of African American Warrant Officers where there had been no prior mention. He was also one of the first (if not the only) warrant officer serving as a regular contributor to the Rocket Newsletter submitting similar works. Chiles has had many "firsts" as evident from his long list of accolades. As if serving a distinctive career spanning almost four decades before retiring as Chief Warrant Officer Four was not enough, Chiles has never been a person who rest on his laurels.

In 2010, his first published book, *As BIG As It Gets*, Chiles chronicles his tenure as the Board Chair of Blacks In Government (BIG), the leading international organization for African-American public service employees. He presents his experiences, observations, and insight into leading BIG during an unprecedented period of growth. The story begins with his election on the Board of Directors and follows his journey to his election as the Chairman of the Board for five consecutive terms.

In 2014, recognizing there were no publications of documented stories of African Americans who served in the Warrant Officer Corps from WWII to the present, Chiles compiled all of his research writings and notes from interviews to pen his second book, *African American Warrant Officers - In Service to Our Country*. A must read, this book highlights those unsung warrant officers who served our country both in and out of uniform from WWII to present.

As a researcher and PhD student, I found his work intriguing, and I wanted to learn more. With that, it was April 2017 that I had the distinct pleasure of conducting a phone interview with Chiles inquiring about his Army experiences as a Vietnam War draftee. Having read all of his published articles, I wanted to capture his thoughts of serving as an African American Soldier. I was also curious about his take on meritocracy as he navigated his career in the Army Warrant Officer Corps. I was very impressed with his recall of his military service, as well as his continued pursuit for excellence in the various assignments throughout his distinguished military career. Our shared appreciation of the American bald eagle and its symbolism of freedom had a positive impact to our research collaboration. More questions would soon follow and after 60 minutes into the phone interview, it was clear to me that I had to meet Chiles in person.

September 2017, I made the journey to fly out from Washington, DC to Southern California for a formal meeting with Chiles. It was the best decision I could have made. I had the opportunity to meet other veterans during lunch to capture their stories as well. The respect and appreciation shown to Chiles from the local community was unequal. The Pomona Public Library had on full display the "Chiles' Eagle Collection". This display served as a focal point of the library where visitors could witness the vast collage of our national bird. The highlight of the trip was the photo op with Chiles with an autographed copy of his second book in hand. It was a half day well spent with my fellow "AG" eagle.

Since our meeting, I not only consider Chiles a pioneer, historian, visionary leader and mentor, but a friend as well. My dissertation title, *Career Ascension of African American Men in the Army Warrant Officer Corps* pays homage to the research work of Chiles that began over a decade ago. My dissertation will focus on the motivation and success strategies for African American men who ascended to the highest ranks in the Army Warrant Officer Corps. This would not have been possible without the discovery of Chiles' earlier writings. His work has inspired me to capture those mute voices of African American men who served in the Army Warrant Officer Corps. I look forward to making this scholarly research a part of "our" history for future scholars to review and add to the literature.

July 9, 2018 marks the 100th Birthday of the Army Warrant Officer Corps. The history of African Americans serving the United States Army Warrant Officer Corps is a long and proud one. As such, we are solely responsible for the narratives we create for ourselves. African American Warrant Officers have performed significant roles in the history of the Warrant Officer Cohort. After a century of service, our achievements and contributions have been widely recognized (in large part due to Chiles), but have not been published. That is until now! Chiles has provided the reader a "master class" of African American Warrant Officer contributions, both past and present. The significance of this period in history could not be timelier. This piece of work should be part of every home library across the globe. *African American Warrant Officer - Their Remarkable History* is "our" blueprint of the African American military experience serving the Warrant Officer Corps in all capacities and at all levels, including Department of the Army, Joint Staff, and the Department of Defense.

Farrell Chiles has captured the alpha and the omega of our truth in military service. As African Americans, we have been the quietest of the "Quiet Professionals" for far too long. This book has now cemented our place in history for generations to come. Well done, Chiles … well done!

CW5 James J. Williams, PhD(c), USAR
Researcher & Scholar-Practitioner
Author, *Chasing The Eagle: From Dreaming To Achieving Success*
& Freedom
March 4, 2018

Introduction

The idea to do this follow-up book to *African American Warrant Officers…In Service to Our Country* came to me while I was attending an annual conference of the Military Writers Society of America in San Antonio in September 2017. I had not planned to write a Volume II, but I was inspired by other writers at the conference and their zeal to tell the stories of the military, fact and fiction, as it related to their experiences, backgrounds, and interests.

As African Americans, we must continue to tell our stories and history too. Thus, in conjunction with the 100th anniversary of the Warrant Officer Cohort, I present "African American Warrant Officers – Their Remarkable History".

Again, I have missed a lot of my fellow African American Army Warrant Officers. Their absence from the book does not take away from their contributions and achievements. It means that I was not able to connect with them or their relatives.

My first book was a result of a lot of research and surfing the internet for historical and background information. However, this book relies primarily on African American Warrant Officers providing information about themselves and their willingness to share their biographies, stories, photos, contributions, and achievements in the military and in their civilian life.

I am honored to present their history. I hope you are inspired by their accomplishments.

"Until the lions have their own historians, the history of the hunt will always glorify the hunter"

-- African Proverb

What is a Warrant Officer?

For those readers unfamiliar with Warrant Officers, this chapter provides the definition of a Warrant Officer, the different grades and ranks, and courses conducted in the Warrant Officer Education System.

Definition

The Army Warrant Officer is an adaptive technical expert, combat leader, trainer, and advisor. Through progressive levels of expertise in assignments, training, and education, the Warrant Officer administers, manages, maintains, operates, and integrates Army systems and equipment across the full spectrum of Army operations. Warrant Officers are formally addressed as either Mr. or Ms.

Warrant Officer 1 (WO1)

Appointed by warrant from the Secretary of the Army. WO1s are technically and tactically focused officers who perform the primary duties of technical leader, trainer, operator, manager, maintainer, sustainer, and advisor.

Chief Warrant Officer 2 (CW2)

Chief Warrant Officers become commissioned officers as provided by the President of the United States. CW2s are intermediate level technical and tactical experts who perform increased duties and responsibilities at the detachment through battalion levels.

Chief Warrant Officer 3 (CW3)

Advanced-level experts who perform the primary duties that of a technical and tactical leader. They provide direction, guidance, resources, assistance, and supervision necessary for subordinates to perform their duties. CW3s primarily support operations levels from team or detachment through brigade.

Chief Warrant Officer 4 (CW4)

Senior-level experts in their chosen field. They primarily support battalion, brigade, division, corps, and echelons above corps operations. CW4s typically have special mentorship responsibilities for other WOs and provide essential advice to commanders on WO issues.

Chief Warrant Officer 5 (CW5)

Master-level technical and tactical experts who support brigade, division, corps, echelons above corps, and major command operations. They provide leader development, mentorship, advice, and counsel to

WOs and branch officers. CW5s have special WO leadership and representation responsibilities within their respective commands.

There are 44 Warrant Officer specialties in 17 different branches.

Warrant Officer Courses

- Warrant Officer Candidate School (WOCS)
- Warrant Officer Basic Course (WOBC)
- Warrant Officer Advanced Course (WOAC)
- Warrant Officer Intermediate Level Education (WOILE)
- Warrant Officer Senior Service Education (WOSSE)
- Training, Advising, and Counseling (TAC)

100th Year Anniversary Observation

Warrant Officers' 100th Celebration!!!

"A Century of Service"

1918 – 2018

The official birthday of the Army Warrant Officers Cohort is July 9, 1918. Prior to that time, Warrant Officers were not commissioned officers, but in reality, were considered civilians. The Judge Advocate General later determined that Warrant Officers held military status.

An Act of Congress on 9 July 1918 documented the founding of the Warrant Officer Corps in the Army by establishing the Army Mine Planter Service as part of the Coast Artillery Corps. Implementation of the Act by the Army was published in the War Department Bulletin 43, dated 22 July 1918.

Highlights of the first one hundred years include:
- On May 12, 1921, a distinctive insignia consisting of an eagle rising with wings, was approved for Warrant Officers.
- In 1941, Public Law 230 authorized appointments up to one percent of the total Regular Army enlisted strength. This law also established two pay rates for Warrant Officers, Warrant Officer Junior Grade (W-1) and Chief Warrant Officer (W-2).
- With the activation of the 99th Pursuit Squadron (March 15, 1941) and with the forming of the 66th Army Air Forces Flight Training Detachment (July 1941), African American Warrant Officers performed in key positions, contributing to the success of their organizations, and making a significant impact on the heritage and legacy of the Tuskegee Airmen.
- In January 1944, the appointment of women as Warrant Officers was authorized.

- During 1948 and 1949, competitive examinations were held to appoint or select for appointment approximately 6,000 regular Army Warrant Officers.
- In 1949, the Career Compensation Act brought about two new pay rates for Warrant Officers. The designations of Warrant Officer Junior Grade (WOJG) and Chief Warrant Officer (CWO) were retained; the grade of Chief Warrant Officer was expanded with the addition of pay grades of W3 and W4.
- In April 1960, the Warrant Officer Program was outlined in Department of the Army Circular 611-7. This document covered utilization policies, criteria for selection, and instruction for conversion to the then new Warrant Officer Military Occupational Specialty (MOS) system.
- In 1966, the Army conducted a review of Warrant Officer career progression and the first Warrant Officer Professional Development Program was published in Department of the Army Pamphlet 600-11.
- The United States Army Warrant Officers Association (USAWOA was founded in 1972.
- In August 1985, the final report of the Department of the Army Total Warrant Officer Study (TWOS) was forwarded to the Army Chief of Staff. This first-ever DA comprehensive analysis of the Total Army warrant officer program provided the opportunity to capture current strengths of the program and build upon those to develop management and training systems that focused on the Army of the 90's and beyond.
- In February 1992, the Warrant Officer Management Act (WOMA) provisions went into effect.
- On October 1, 1992, the first active Army Chief Warrant Officer was promoted to CW5.
- In 1996, a U.S. Army Warrant Officers History Book was undertaken by the United States Army Warrant Officers Association to tell the story of the Corps.
- In September 1999, the Chief of Staff, Army, chartered the Army Development System (ADS) XXI Task Force to examine

the Enlisted and Warrant Officer Personnel Management Systems.

- May 23, 2001 was the first time a Warrant Officer was presented with the prestigious General Douglas MacArthur Leadership Award.
- On July 18, 2002, the Army Training and Leader Development Panel Reports on the Warrant Officer Study. The Report and recommendations were released on August 22, 2002 after approval by the Chief of Staff and Secretary of the Army.
- On March 28, 2003, the United States Army Warrant Officers Association Scholarship Foundation was incorporated in the Commonwealth of Virginia.
- The Warrant Officer Historical Foundation was founded on May 29, 2003.
- On January 1, 2006, the book "WARRANT – The Legacy of Leadership as a Warrant Officer" was published.
- From June 7 to 11, 2010, the first Warrant Officer Summit was held at the U. S. Army Warrant Officer Career College (WOCC), Fort Rucker, Alabama.
- In 2011, the first Warrant Officer graduated from the National Defense University, better known as the "War College".
- On March 14, 2014, the Chief of Staff, Army (CSA), created a new position for an Army Staff Senior Warrant Officer (ARSTAF SWO).
- On June 10, 2015, MILPER Message 15-166 announced the initial MOS 170A Warrant Officer Cyber Branch Voluntary Transfer for Active Duty Warrants.
- On June 26, 2017, the first African American Warrant Officer was inducted into the Order of the Eagle Rising Society joining a group of nineteen other distinguished Warrant Officers.
- The above information was gathered from the Warrant Officer Historical Foundation – https://warrantofficerhistory.org.

One Hundred Years and still going strong.

African Americans in the Warrant Officer Cohort

African American Warrant Officers have performed significant roles in the history of the Warrant Officer Cohort. Their achievements and contributions have been widely recognized.

Harry H. Hollowell joined the Tenth Calvary (Buffalo Soldiers) as a private in January 1936. He served in the Army for twenty eight years, retiring as a Chief Warrant Officer Four and bandleader in August 1964. On July 19, 2009, "Hollowell Drive" was dedicated in his honor at Fort Leavenworth, Kansas.

Cleveland Valrey joined the Army Air Corps in at the age of 16 in 1949. He was the first African American inducted into the United States Army Aviation Hall of Fame. CW4 Valrey was also inducted into the United States Army Ranger Hall of Fame.

Harrison E. Robinson is a member of the Ordnance Corps Hall of Fame. Mr. Robinson entered the Army as an inductee in 1946. CW4 Robinson died in 1978. In August 2013, the CW4 Harrison E. Robinson Ordnance School Conference Room was dedicated in his honor at the Ordnance School at Fort Lee, Virginia.

Carl Burhanan served in the Army for 26 years. His combat experience included Korea and Vietnam. Mr. Burhanan graduated in Flight Class 55-4. He flew 9,024 hours and 332 combat hours. His decorations include the Presidential Service Medal and eight Air Medals. CW4 (Retired) Burhanan was the first African American to become a Presidential Aircraft Commander.

Carl E. Black entered the Army in September 1953 and completed Basic Airborne School at Fort Bragg, North Carolina in 1956. He later became a Legal Administrator. Mr. Black retired in October 1974. For his exemplary service, CW4 Black was made the Honorary Regimental Warrant Officer of the Judge Advocate General Corps.

Robert Levi "Bob" Wimberly joined the Army in 1959. He was promoted to CW5 on January 23, 1999. Mr. Wimberly became the first African American appointed to the position of State Command Chief Warrant Officer (New Jersey) in the Army National guard of the United States.

Mary F. Carter was the first female to serve on the Board of Directors of the United States Army Warrant Officers Association. Additionally, she was the first female Warrant Officer honored as the CW4 Albert M. Holcombe Warrant Officer of the Year in 1984. She retired as a Chief Warrant Officer Five.

Eddie Mallard joined the Army in 1965 and retired in 2009. Mr. Mallard served as the Command Chief Warrant Officer of the United States Intelligence and Security Command (INSCOM) from June 2004 to August 2009. He serves on the Board of Directors and as Treasurer of the United States Army Warrant Officers Association's Scholarship Foundation.

Aurelia "Vicki" Murray served in the National Guard. Ms. Murray joined the Air National Guard in Ohio in June 1973. She became the first African female Warrant Officer in the Ohio National Guard as a WO1 in March 1978. Ms. Murray became the first African American woman promoted in the Army to CW5 on November 4, 1999.

Douglas Vincent Clapp entered the Army on August 8, 1974. He was appointed as a Warrant Officer on January 31, 1985. On November 29, 2004, he made the ultimate sacrifice when he died in a non-hostile incident at the age of 49. CW5 Clapp served in Desert Storm and Operation Iraqi Freedom. The Douglas Vincent Clapp Memorial Conference Center at Fort Hood, Texas is named in his honor.

Jonathan W. Hosley, as an enlisted Soldier, was injured by an improvised explosive device in Iraq in November 2004, and lost his left leg below the knee. He later submitted an application to become a Warrant Officer. He was selected for the program and became the first-ever amputee to complete the Army Warrant Officer Candidate School.

Coral J. Jones enlisted in the Army on November 24, 1981. She was appointed a WO1 on August 19, 1994. On October 1, 2010, Ms. Jones made Army history when she became the first African American female to earn the rank of chief warrant officer five within the active Army Adjutant General Corps. CW5 Jones assumed the duties as the Chief Warrant Officer of the Adjutant General Corps on February 17, 2011 (the fifth CWO of the Army AG Corps).

David Williams entered Active Duty in July 1977. He completed Warrant Officer Candidate School and Flight Training in 1987. His combat tours included serving as the Senior Warrant Officer and Warrant Officer Advisor to the Multi-National Force-Iraq Commanding General. On March 14, 2014, the Chief of Staff Army (CSA) selected CW5 Williams as the first ARSTAF Senior Warrant Officer (SWO).

Rufus Montgomery, Sr. began his military career as an enlisted soldier in 1965. CW5 Montgomery retired in 2003. In July 2015, a corridor located within the Warrant Officer Technical College, Army Logistics University, was dedicated in his honor. Mr. Montgomery was inducted into the Order of Eagle Rising Society in June 2017, making him the first African American to receive the honor. He joined a distinguished group of nineteen other Warrant Officers in the society.

Lawrence Blackwell joined the Army in 1979. He was appointed a Warrant Officer in 1990. CW5 Blackwell was attached to the 1st Armor Division during Operation Iraqi Freedom and supported over 2,000 tracked and wheeled vehicles organized for combat operations. He directly contributed to the 97% operations readiness rate for the Brigade Combat Team while deployed in a combat zone. Chief

Warrant Officer Five Blackwell retired in 2011. In 2017, Mr. Blackwell was inducted into the United States Army Ordnance Hall of Fame.

* * *

These individuals represent just a small sampling of African American Warrant Officers who have made an impact in the history of the Warrant Officer Cohort. There are many more.

African American Warrant Officers...In Service to Our Country

Written by Farrell J. Chiles, CW4 (Retired), USA

(Originally Published in the Rocket Newsletter – Spring 2015)

In 2005, I wrote my first article on African American Warrants Officers. Since that time, I have written over a dozen articles on African American Warrant Officers, some which have appeared in the ROCKET.

My research has led me on an adventure to find as much information possible on African American Warrant Officers. The culmination of the articles, research, interviews, and quest for information, has led me to write a book on the history, achievements, and contributions of African American Warrant Officers in and out of the military. The book was released in January 2015 and is entitled "African American Warrant Officers...In Service to Our Country". The book is available at www.booklocker.com, barnesandnoble.com, and amazon.com.

For Black History Month 2015, I would like to share two profiles from the book:

Carl M. Burnett

Carl Burnett is the Chief Executive Officer (CEO) of Geocode-LA, Inc., a privately held company with 51-200 employees in the Information Services Industry.

Geocode-LA, Inc. is the provider of a global standard for Geospatial Point Representation. The company sells geospatial information products and services. The patented Geocode® algorithm is a standard essential patent (SEP) for many industrial applications. It creates a singular geospatial coordinate for global point location identification.

From January 2007 – December 2012, he served as an Adjunct faculty member at Montgomery Community College at the Information Technology Institute. From September 2004 – December 2012, Burnett was a part-time practitioner faculty for undergraduate and graduate information technology programs in the Johns Hopkins University Carey Business School.

Burnett received a Master of Science (MS), Information Technology and a Bachelor of Science from the John Hopkins University Carey Business School.

Mr. Burnett retired from the Army as a Chief Warrant Officer Four. During his military career, he served on the Department of the Army Total Warrant Officer Study (TWOS).

Carl Burnett served as the United States Army Warrant Officers Association's National President from 1976 – 1978. He is the first and only, so far, African American to hold that position.

Dr. Harry L. Hobbs

Dr. Harry L. Hobbs is the spokesperson for the Huntsville (Alabama) Utilities. Prior to his current position, Dr. Hobbs was the Communications Relations Officer for four years with the Huntsville Police Department (HPD).

CW5 Hobbs retired from the military in 2007. In November 2013, he was inducted into the U.S. Army Ordnance Hall of Fame. In December 2013, he was inducted into the Warrant Officer Eagle Rising Society, which recognizes the lifetime achievements of a Warrant Officer.

Dr. Hobbs has a Doctorate Degree in Human Resource Management from Pacific Western University, a Master of Science Degree in Human Services, Murray State University, and a Bachelor of Science degree in Resource Management from Troy State University.

In January 2014, Dr. Hobbs was awarded the 2014 Unity Award during the 29th Martin Luther King Jr. Unity Breakfast sponsored by the Delta Theta Lambda Chapter of the Alpha Phi Alpha fraternity. In March 2014, he was the recipient the 2014 Whitney M. Young Jr. Community Award, established by the Boy Scouts of America.

He is currently pursuing a second Doctorate Ph.D. degree in Business Administration.

Conclusion

The book does not attempt to chronicle every African American Warrant Officer who has served. The book represents a snapshot of some outstanding warrant officers as an example of the achievements and accomplishments that may have been overlooked.

There is an African proverb that says "Until the lions have their own historians, the history of the hunt will always glorify the hunter".

CW4 (Ret) Carl M. Burnett

CW5 (Ret) Harry L. Hobbs

Profile from Warrant Officers' History: Chief Warrant Officer Five (Ret) Rowmell R. Hughes
By CW4 Farrell J. Chiles, USA, Ret.
(Originally Published in the Rocket – Summer 2015)

Rowmell Hughes was born on May 7, 1948 in Bishopville, Lee County, South Carolina. Her parents were the late Booker T. and Luevenia Allen Roary. The daughter of a sharecropper, Rowmell remembers getting up early every morning at 4:00 A.M. to journey to the fields to pick cotton or tobacco. From that early experience, she learned what hard work is and the values of responsibility and accountability.

Chief Warrant Officer Five Rowmell R. Hughes enlisted in the Women's Army Corps in 1970 and upon completion of her active duty commitment, joined the Army Reserve. In 1989, she completed the Warrant Officer Candidate School at Fort McCoy, Wisconsin and the Warrant Officer Tactical/Technical Certification Course at Fort Benjamin Harrison, Indiana. She was then appointed a Warrant Officer One in the Adjutant General Corps. Her initial assignment as a personnel warrant was with the 319th Transportation Brigade in Oakland, California and she later transferred to the 2nd Medical Brigade as a Personnel Management Officer.

In 1993, she became the Supervisory Staff Administrator in the 2nd Medical Brigade. In this dual status civilian capacity, she represented the Commanding General and was responsible for the daily operations of an organization that encompassed seven western states (CA, NV, AZ, MT, CO, UT and Washington). The brigade was comprised of 6,000 soldiers. The position was the highest civilian position in the brigade and Ms. Hughes was the highest ranking African American civilian within the 63d Regional Readiness Command. In October 2002, she received the United States Army's Citation Award for Exceptional Service. The award was presented to Ms. Hughes by the Army Vice Chief of Staff.

Chief Warrant Officer Five Hughes served as a staff officer on various short tours for major Army exercises in CONUS and in Japan, Korea, and Okinawa. In 2004, she was cross-leveled and deployed with the 376th Personnel Service Battalion, from Long Beach, California, in support of Operation Iraqi Freedom in Tikrit, Iraq. While there, she served as the Detachment II Human Resources Technician/Executive Officer at the Forward Operating Base (FOB) in Speicher. During the tour, she and her staff had the responsibility to provide personnel services to the 5,000 Soldiers assigned to five geographical dispersed FOBs in Northern Iraq.

In September 2008, Chief Warrant Officer Hughes was assigned to the G-1 Section, 70th Regional Readiness Command, Fort Lawton, Seattle, Washington. She is a graduate of the Adjutant General Warrant Officer Advance Course, and the Warrant Officer Staff and Senior Courses.

Chief Warrant Officer Five Hughes' military awards include the Legion of Merit, the Meritorious Service Medal with Oak Leaf Cluster, the Army Commendation Medal with Silver Oak Leaf Cluster, the Army Good Conduct Medal, Army Reserve Component Achievement Medal with Silver Oak Leaf Cluster, National Defense Service Medal with Bronze Star, Iraq Campaign Medal, Global War on Terrorism Service Medal, Armed Forces Reserve Medal with hour glass and "M" Device, Noncommissioned Officer Professional Development Ribbon, Army Service Ribbon, and the Overseas Service Ribbon. She is authorized to wear the Superior Service Medal for outstanding service as a civilian. In 2004, Chief Warrant Officer Five Hughes was selected by the California Department of the Reserve Officers Association for the Outstanding Warrant Officer of the Year Award.

In July 2009, Chief Warrant Officer Five Hughes retired from the military with 38 years of service. A resident of Vallejo, California, she is the mother of Romi Weathersby and the grandmother of Nevaeh and Quincy.

* Ms. Hughes died on December 4, 2015.

Profile from Warrant Officers' History: Chief Warrant Officer Five (Ret) James A. Jackson
Written by CW4 Farrell J. Chiles, USA, Ret.
(Originally Published in the ROCKET – Fall 2015)

Chief Warrant Officer Five James A. Jackson was inducted into the Ordnance Hall of Fame on 14 May 2014.

James A. Jackson was born in Greenback, Tennessee on January 21, 1946. His parents were William H. Jackson Jr. and Lelia T. Jackson. His siblings included four brothers – Matthew, Wilburn, Joseph, and Melvin, and three sisters – Annette, Erma, and Mary.

In June 1964, he voluntarily enlisted in the United States Army and completed Basic Training at Fort Gordon, Georgia. He was then assigned to the 504th Signal Company in Mannheim, Germany where he served as a Field Radio Repairman. In October 1980, Sergeant First Class Jackson received a direct appointment to Warrant Officer One as an Electronics Communication Technician and was assigned to the 327th Signal Battalion, Fort Bragg, North Carolina.

From 2000 to 2003, Jackson was assigned to the United States Army Ordnance Munitions and Electronics Maintenance School (OMEMS), Redstone Arsenal, Alabama where he served in positions as the Chief of Administration and Operations Division and Chief, Warrant Officer Training Division. Jackson supervised the training of the Ordnance Corps annual course load for the Warrant Officer Basic Course for Ammunition Technicians, Electronic Systems Maintenance Technicians and Electronic Missile Maintenance Technicians and served as the Warrant Officer Senior training Advisor to the Director of Instruction and the brigade commander and staff.

Mr. Jackson's awards and decorations include the Legion of Merit; Bronze Star Medal; Meritorious Service Medal (5th award); Army Commendation Medal (7th award); Army Achievement Medal; Army Good Conduct Medal (5th award); National Defense Service Medal (3rd award); Southwest Asia Service Medal with Bronze Star (2nd award); Global War on Terrorism Service Medal; Korean Defense Service Medal; Non Commissioned Officer Professional Development Ribbon (3rd award); Amy Service Medal; Overseas Service Ribbon

(10th award); Republic of Vietnam Campaign Medal; Kuwait Liberation Medal (Saudi Arabia); and Kuwait Liberation Medal (Kuwait).

Chief Warrant Officer Five Jackson culminated his career with his assignment to the 5th Signal Command's G4 Support Operations Division to support highly sensitive missions directed by the Joint Chiefs of Staff and US Army Europe.

CW5 James Jackson retired on 1 March 2008 after serving over 43 years of continuous federal active service. He was the longest serving 918E Communications and Electronics Maintenance Technician in the history of the Army. He considers his most significant achievement was serving as the Chief of the Warrant Officer Training Division from January 2002 until January 2004 at the Redstone Arsenal in Huntsville, Alabama.

Reflecting on his military career, Mr. Jackson said, "I entered the Army on 8 June 1964 and attended Basic Radio Repair School. It opened up a new world. It was the basis for the steps I would take to achieve what I am today. Today, I am a retired CW5 Senor Electronics Maintenance Technician, after serving 43 years, eight months, and 23 days of honorable military service". Mr. Jackson is quoted as saying, "My motto is look like a Soldier, act like a Soldier, and perform like a Soldier. What you put in life is what you get out of it".

CW5 Jackson currently resides in Whites Creek, Tennessee with his wife Joanne P. Jackson. They have two adult daughters – Denise Jackson Hill and Careasa Jackson Greer.

Mr. Jackson's past time is restoring old automobiles. He has a 1970 Mustang; a 1953 Ford F100 truck; and a 1937 Chevrolet.

CW5 (Ret) James A. Jackson

Profile from Warrant Officers' History:
Chief Warrant Officer Four (Retired) Percy Dean Butler
Written by CW4 Farrell J. Chiles, USA, Ret.
(Originally Published in the ROCKET – Spring 2016)

Percy Dean Butler was born in Pritchard, Mobile, Alabama on December 28, 1943 and was raised in Pritchard, Alabama and Gulfport, Mississippi. He graduated from Thirty-Third Avenue High School, Gulfport, Mississippi and attended college at Los Angeles City College and the University of California at Los Angeles (UCLA) before enlisting in the Army in May 1964.

Chief Warrant Officer Butler's twenty year Army career was spent specializing in Human Resources, Personnel Administration and Management; Staff Combat Operations and Planning; and, Analysis. During his military, he earned a Bachelor of Science Degree in Business Administration awarded by American Technological University and pursued his post graduate work in Master of Science Business Administration (MSBA) with Boston University's European Campus. Not one to sit idle, he consistently progressed in rank to become a Chief Warrant Officer Four, serving in various posts in the United States, Republic of West Germany, and two combat tours to the Republic of Vietnam. He earned the Bronze Star Medal (2 awards), the Meritorious Service Medal (2 awards) and other awards and decorations.

After retiring from the military on 1 November 1984, Mr. Butler began to search for opportunities to successfully utilize his management background and training. Butler decided to offer his services to the public and successfully launched his own financial consulting and insurance business in the Greater Atlanta area. He is the President and Founder of The Advantage Capital Group, Inc., Atlanta, Georgia.

Percy Dean Butler is recognized as a leader/innovator in the financial management and insurance profession. His professional and personal philosophies are simple: If you want to help yourself, you must first help others, and if you want results, you have to make them happen". Mr. Butler's life has been dedicated to proving that motto and is reflected throughout his careers, which have included more than twenty years of distinguished and honorable service as a military officer, and the development and nurturing of a privately owned financial corporation. In his personal life, he shares his philosophy by participating in the coaching/mentoring of those desiring to further their education in school or business, public speaking engagements, and by providing estate and financial planning seminars.

CW4 Butler has devoted a great deal of his time and has been active throughout the continental United States, serving as a Presidential Appointee on the Veterans Administration Advisory Committee on National Cemeteries and Memorial where he was elected to serve as Vice Chairman and Chairman for more than four years. Mr. Butler served as the European Region President of the United States Army Warrant Officer Association from 1980-1981 and on the National Board of Directors from 1982-1985. He served as Assistant Vice President for Veterans Affairs and is a Life Member of the Unites States Army Warrant Officers Association; Member of Veterans of Foreign Wars; and the American Legion. In 2014, he was inducted as a Distinguished Member of the Regiment (DMOR) in the Adjutant General Corps. He has been active in the NAACP, the former Atlanta Exchange, and numerous business and civic organizations within the community. Mr. Butler is Co-Founder of The Business Forum of Atlanta, Inc. He is a Mason, 32nd Degree and Shriner.

Percy Butler is married to the former Patsy Ruth Munford and the proud father of three sons, Staff Sergeant Kevin Dean Butler (completed 17+ years of service), Major (Retired) Karel Alan Butler, and Keith Eric. Percy is immensely proud of his grandchildren, Julian Dean, Jourdain Alexander, Kayin Sherelle, and Lauryan Patrice Butler.

CW4 (Ret) Percy D. Butler

Profile from Warrant Officers' History:
Chief Warrant Officer Five (Retired)
Ida Tyree-Hyche
Submitted by CW4 Farrell J. Chiles, USA, Ret.
(Originally Published in the ROCKET – Fall 2016)

After 35 years of serving her country well as an Army Reserve Soldier, a mobilized Soldier in support of Operations Iraqi and Enduring Freedom, and a civil servant Human Resources leader for the Department of the Army, throughout the 121st U.S. Army Reserve Command (USARCOM), 81st Regional Support Command (RSC) serving eight southeastern states; Third U.S. Army Central Command (USARCENT) Special Troops Battalion, Fort McPherson, Georgia; 310th AG Group, Fort Jackson, South Carolina; 3rd Personnel Command (PERSCOM), Jackson, Mississippi; 87th Division East, Vestavia, Alabama; and the 108th Training Division's subordinate command at Fort Gillem, GA, Ida Tyree-Hyche retired at the top rank of Chief Warrant Officer Five (CW5), in 2011.

The following year, having completed over 30 years in human resource management leadership for the Department of the Army federal agency in Birmingham, Alabama, Vestavia, Alabama, and Huntsville, Alabama, Ms. Tyree-Hyche closed the federal civil servant chapter of her life under the Army Materiel Command (AMC) at Redstone Arsenal, Alabama, to begin her legal career by opening up her own law practice. The practice, now a partnership with her daughter, Attorney Shade' A. Dixon, named Tyree Hyche & Dixon, LLC, serves Alabama and Georgia.

One of less than ten African American female warrant officers to achieve the highest rank for a warrant officer during her Army Reserve career in the Adjutant General Corps, Chief Warrant Officer Tyree-Hyche served as a reserve warrant officer on active duty during Operations Iraqi and Enduring Freedom as Deputy Adjutant for Third U.S. Army Central Command, Special Troops Battalion in Fort McPherson, Georgia and Camp Arifjan, Kuwait, Southwest Asia. She further served as Adjutant for the Warrior Transition Battalion at Fort Benning, Georgia, before ending her mobilization tour.

As a CW3, The Reserve Officers Association (ROA) selected her as the ROA Warrant Officer of the Year for the Year 2000, among three finalists who appeared before a board in Washington, D.C. An avid writer, Tyree-Hyche published several articles in the ROA Officer Magazine and the United States Army Warrant Officers Association (USAWOA) Newsliner. She served as the first female warrant officer to lead the Southeastern Region of the United States Army Warrant Officers Association, serving chapters in Alabama, Georgia, Tennessee, South Carolina, North Carolina, Florida, and Puerto Rico. In that role, Tyree-Hyche was also a member of the Board of Directors of the USAWOA. She also served as the first African American female to lead her local chapter of the Reserve Officers Association in Birmingham, Alabama. For a short period of time, CW5 Tyree-Hyche served as the first African American female warrant officer on the Board of Directors for the Warrant Officer Historical Foundation.

"I cherish memories of my military career. It infused a sense of service; service, not only to my country, but to others," Tyree-Hyche said. "I believe we grow and develop a strong quality of life by building communities of service to others so self-less service completes me."

Upon retirement, Tyree-Hyche brought her skills and commitment to service as an attorney. She is managing partner of Tyree Hyche & Dixon, LLC, a firm that practices workers compensation, probate, and employment law (Title VII of the Civil Rights Act) in Alabama and Trademark, Copyright, & business development in Georgia. Tyree-Hyche, in her role of attorney, overcame the United States Patent and Trademark Office's finding of "likelihood of confusion" with an existing organization's trademark to successfully trademarking the USAWOA brand, "*Quiet Professionals*".

Ms. Tyree-Hyche was recognized by the Birmingham Bar Association (BBA) in 2014 for her pro bono service to persons who least can afford legal services through the BBA Pro Bono Award for Extended Representation Attorney in District Court. In 2016, she was named to the Board of the Birmingham Volunteer Lawyers Program. Also in 2016, she completed her term as President of the League of

Women Voters of Greater Birmingham and member of the State Board of the League of Women Voters of Alabama.

Author of the book, <u>Bar Studies Inspiration,</u> written after retirement and published in 2013, Tyree-Hyche declares, "Some people say I don't know how to retire fully. I say there is life after retirement, and it is BETTER."

CW5 Ida Tyree-Hyche

Attorney Ida Tyree-Hyche

Profile from Warrant Officers' History:
Chief Warrant Officer Five James J. Williams
By Farrell J. Chiles, CW4, USA, Retired
(Originally Published in the ROCKET - Spring 2017)

Chief Warrant Officer Five James J. Williams, a native of Cleveland Ohio, was born on 30 August, 1964. He enlisted in the Army Reserve on 19 September 1988 as a Private First Class (PFC) in the Adjutant General Corps. He is an IMA reservist currently assigned to the Pentagon serving as the J4-JLOC Action Officer for the Joint Chiefs of Staff. A Fast Track Program selectee, Williams completed Basic Training and Advance Administration training at Fort Jackson in May 1989. He was mobilized to support Operation Desert Storm from January to April 1991 at McGuire AFB, New Jersey. Following his mobilization, Williams remained an enlisted service member achieving the rank of E-5 in 1993.

On 7 August 1998, Mr. Williams completed Warrant Officer Candidate (WOC) School at Fort Rucker, Alabama, and was appointed to the rank of WO1 before reporting to his new assignment with the US Joint Forces Command (JFCOM) in Norfolk, Virginia. He continued serving in the AG Corps as a 420A. In December 2001, Mr. Williams was mobilized to JFCOM for a 730-day assignment in support of OEF/OIF. He served as the Computer Network Defense Action Officer in the J-6 Directorate. Post 9/11, he served as the J-3 Reserve Affairs Officer.

On 30 October 2008, with more than 20 years of service, Chief Warrant Officer Williams accepted a new position in the Drilling Individual Mobilization Augmentation (DIMA) program assigned to the US Pacific Command (PACOM) at Camp Smith, Hawaii. He later served a 36-month deployment to PACOM's Joint Cyber Center Pacific (CYBERPAC) supporting cyberspace operations covering Japan, South Korea, and the Philippines. Following that assignment, Mr. Williams completed a 179-day tour supporting HQDA-Office of the Inspector General in Arlington, VA.

EDUCATION

A huge advocate of higher education, Chief Warrant Officer Williams holds a Bachelor's degree in Computer Information Systems and a Master's degree in Public Administration. He is currently pursuing a PhD in Public Management and Leadership from Walden University. His dissertation topic: *Rising Above the Frey: A Phenomenological Study of African American Males' Career Ascension To Senior Field Grade Warrant Officer Status In The Army.* Williams completed all military education including the Warrant Officer Intermediate Level Education (WOILE) and the Warrant Officer Senior Service Education (WOSSE).

AWARDS, DECORATIONS, AND RECOGNITION

CW5 Williams' military decoration and awards include the Defense Meritorious Service Medal, Joint Service Commendation Medal, Army Commendation Medal (OLC), Joint Service Achievement Medal (OLC), Army Achievement Medal, Army Reserve Components Achievement Medal (9th OLC), Global War on Terrorism Service Medal, and the Joint Meritorious Unit Award (OLC).

CIVILIAN OCCUPATION

As a Citizen-Soldier, Chief Warrant Officer Williams is dual careered in the private sector and academia. He is a Senior Cyber Information Assurance Analyst with Northrop Grumman Corporation. Mr. Williams is also an Associate Adjunct Instructor at the University of Phoenix. In the School of Business, Mr. Williams facilitates undergraduate courses including, *Innovative Leadership*, *Business Communications*, and *Managing Change in the Workplace*.

PROFESSIONAL PUBLICATIONS

Mr. Williams is the Publisher/CEO of Rising Eagle Publishing, LLC, an independent, veteran-owned publishing company in Mitchellville, Maryland. An award-winning author of his debut book, *CHASING THE EAGLE: From Dreaming to Achieving Success & Freedom*, and best-selling co-author of his second book, *MISSION*

UNSTOPPABLE: Extraordinary Stories of Failure's Blessings, CW5 Williams shares his personal story of success and achievement that has equally inspired students, corporate executives, and military leaders.

Chief Warrant Officer Five Williams is husband to the former Greta Bolden of Washington, DC. They are also proud parents to their son – James II.

CW5 James J. Williams

African American Warrant Officers...In Service to Our Country

By Farrell J. Chiles, CW4 (Retired), USA

(Originally Published in the USAWOA Newsliner – February 2015)

In 2005, I wrote my first article on African American Warrants Officers. Since that time, I have written over a dozen articles on African American Warrant Officers, many which have appeared in the Newsliner.

My research has led me on an adventure to find as much information possible on African American Warrant Officers. The culmination of the articles, research, interviews, and quest for information, has led me to write a book on the history, achievements, and contributions of African American Warrant Officers in and out of the military. The book was released in January 2015, and is entitled "African American Warrant Officers...In Service to Our Country". The book is available at www.booklocker.com, Amazon.com and Barnes and Noble.com.

For Black History Month 2015, I would like to share three profiles from the book:

Carl M. Burnett

Carl Burnett is the Chief Executive Officer (CEO) of Geocode-LA, Inc., a privately held company 51-200 employees in the Information Services Industry.

Geocode-LA, Inc. is the provider of a global standard for Geospatial Point Representation. The company sells geospatial information products and services. The patented Geocode® algorithm is a standard essential patent (SEP) for many industrial applications. It creates a singular geospatial coordinate for global point location identification.

From January 2007 – December 2012, he served as an Adjunct faculty member at Montgomery Community College at the Information Technology Institute. From September 2004 – December 2012, Burnett was a part-time practitioner faculty for undergraduate and graduate information technology programs in the Johns Hopkins

University Carey Business School. Graduate and undergraduate teaching concentrations included Information Systems (design, development, implementation, maintenance, and analysis); E-Commerce; Project Management; Internet Multimedia; Computer Program Design; Service Oriented Architecture and Blue Ocean Strategy. Graduate program teaching concentrations include Information Security Architecture and Assurance; E-Commerce Security; and Service Oriented Architecture Security.

Burnett received a Master of Science (MS), Information Technology and a Bachelor of Science from the John Hopkins University Carey Business School.

Mr. Burnett retired from the Army as a Chief Warrant Officer Four. During his military career, he served on the Department of the Army Total Warrant Officer Study (TWOS).

Carl Burnett served as the United States Army Warrant Officers Association's National President from 1976 – 1978. He is the first and only, so far, African American to hold that position.

Dr. Harry L. Hobbs

Dr. Harry L. Hobbs is the spokesperson for the Huntsville Utilities. Prior to his current position, Dr. Hobbs was the Communications Relations Officer for four years with the Huntsville Police Department (HPD).

CW5 Hobbs retired from the military in 2007. In November 2013, he was inducted into the U.S. Army Ordnance Hall of Fame. In December 2013, he was inducted into the Warrant Officer Eagle Rising Society, which recognizes the lifetime achievements of a Warrant Officer.

Dr. Hobbs has a Doctorate Degree in Human Resource Management from Pacific Western University, a Master of Science Degree in Human Services, Murray State University, and a Bachelor of Science degree in Resource Management from Troy State University.

Dr. Hobbs was selected as the Mentor of the Year 2011 for the City of Huntsville by the 100 Black Men of Greater Huntsville Chapter. He was selected as the Veteran of the Year 2012 for City of

Madison by the Madison City Rotary Club. He was also recognized by Congressman Mo Brooks for being selected as the Madison City Outstanding Veteran 2012 for his service to veterans and the community.

In January 2014, Dr. Hobbs was awarded the 2014 Unity Award during the 29th Martin Luther King Jr. Unity Breakfast sponsored by the Delta Theta Lambda chapter of the Alpha Phi Alpha fraternity. In March 2014, he was the recipient the 2014 Whitney M. Young Jr. Community Award, established by the Boy Scouts of America.

He is currently pursuing a second Doctorate Ph.D. degree Business Administration.

Octavia G. Saine, Executive Officer, National Oceanic and Atmospheric Administration (NOAA) Office of General Counsel

Octavia G. Saine, CW3(R), US Army JAG Corps, joined the National Oceanic and Atmospheric (NOAA) Office of General Counsel as the Executive Officer in June 2010. Prior to joining NOAA, she served as the Deputy for Financial Management and Public Outreach for the Eisenhower Memorial Commission from 2008 to 2010.

After retirement from the US Army JAG Corps in 2004, she held various leadership positions in the private sector in the Washington, D.C. metro area and Charlotte, North Carolina. Most notably, Federal Home Management Corporation (Freddie Mac), Bank of America, and Charlotte Mecklenburg County Schools.

Octavia has received several awards since her retirement from the Army JAG Corps such as Bank of America's Award of Excellence and Sprit Award, and the Department of Commerce Office of General Counsel Distinguished Employee award for 2013.

Octavia's twenty-year career with the U.S. Army culminated at the U.S. Army Legal Services Agency where she served as the Chief Legal Administrator.

Octavia received her undergraduate degree in 1981 from Winston-Salem State University, Winston-Salem, North Carolina and her graduate degree from Webster University, St. Louis, Missouri, in 1993.

She lives in Springfield, Virginia with her husband Tim Saine and their daughter, Alisha.

Conclusion

The book does not attempt to chronicle every African American Warrant Officer who has served. The book represents a snapshot of some outstanding warrant officers as an example of the achievements and accomplishments that may have been overlooked.

There is an African proverb that says "Until the lions have their own historians, the history of the hunt will always glorify the hunter".

CW4 (Ret) Carl M. Burnett

CW5 (Ret) Harry L. Hobbs

CW3 (Ret) Octavia Saine

African American Warrant Officers and the Army Ordnance Corps
Hall of Fame
By CW4 (Ret) Farrell J. Chiles
(Originally Published in the USAWOA Newsliner –February 2016)

Background

The Ordnance Branch was founded on 14 May 1812, making it one of the oldest branches in the United States Army. The branch is currently located at Fort Lee, Virginia. Prior to its move to Fort Lee, the branch, for over a century, was located at Aberdeen Proving Ground in Maryland.

The U.S. Ordnance Corps' mission is to support the development, production, acquisition, and sustainment of weapon systems, ammunition, missiles, electronics, and ground mobility material during peace and war to provide combat power for the U.S. Army.

Warrant Officer Military Occupational Specialties in the Ordnance Branch consist of 890A, 913A, 914A, 915A, 915E, 919A, 948B, 948D, and 948E.

The Army Ordnance Corps Hall of Fame

The Army Ordnance Corps Hall of Fame was established in 1969 to recognize and memorialize persons who have made a positive, significant contribution to the U.S. Army Ordnance Corps.

The individuals are chosen solely on their significant contribution to the Corps and each selectee is able to stand up to close scrutiny. "Attainment of high rank or position is not necessarily indicative of a significant contribution to Ordnance. Likewise, rank, sec, ethnicity and/or religion are not discriminators."

Currently, there are 46 warrant officers in the Hall of Fame. The first was inducted in 1981. The first African American warrant officer was inducted in 1991. There are nine African American warrant officers in the Hall of Fame, representing 19.6% of the warrant officers inducted into the Hall.

Chief Warrant Officer Four Harrison E. Robinson

Chief Warrant Officer Harrison E. Robinson was inducted into the Hall of Fame in 1991.

Harrison Robinson was born in Atlantic City, New Jersey in 1927 and entered the Army as an inductee in 1946.

Mr. Robinson rose to the rank of master sergeant and served as a battalion maintenance sergeant in several units and as a noncommissioned officer in charge of heavy equipment and wheel vehicles for the 782nd Maintenance Battalion of the 82nd Airborne Division.

In 1951, he was appointed a Warrant Officer and served as a maintenance officer with a number of units in the United States, Europe, Korea, and Vietnam, including the 82nd and 101st Airborne Divisions. Mr. Robinson retired in 1978 and died later that year.

On October 18, 2013, the U.S. Army Ordnance School at Fort Lee, Virginia hosted a rededication ceremony for the Chief Warrant Officer Four Harrison E. Robinson Conference Room. The conference room was originally dedicated on May 9, 1996 at the former Ordnance School which was located at Aberdeen Proving Grounds, Maryland.

Chief Warrant Officer Four Everett C. Evans, Sr.

Chief Warrant Officer Everett C. Evans was inducted into the Hall of Fame in 1995.

Everett Evans was born in Rossville, Ohio on June 3, 1937. Evans was appointed as a warrant officer in 1965 and assigned as an armament technician to Company C, 703rd Maintenance Battalion, 3rd Infantry Division where he formed control teams to support tank gunnery training in Grafenwohr, West Germany's largest NATO training site.

As an instructor/writer assigned to the Ordnance Center and School, he instructed the first Warrant Officer Entry Course and served as the primary staff officer for the initial development of the Master Mechanic Program.

Mr. Evans retired from the military in 1977 and in 1980 was hired as a training specialist at the Ordnance Center and School. He retired as Assistant Director of Training and Doctrine in 1992. Mr. Evans was selected to serve as Honorary Warrant Officer of the Ordnance Corps in 1988.

Chief Warrant Officer Five Fred Norman

Chief Warrant Officer Fred Norman was inducted into the Hall of Fame in 2005.

Fred Norman was born on September 2, 1935 in Albany, Georgia and enlisted in the Army in 1955. He completed Basic Training at Fort Jackson, South Carolina and following Advanced Individual Training at Fort Knox, Kentucky, served as a mechanic in Germany.

In 1969, Mr. Norman was appointed a warrant officer and assigned to Fort Baker, California, as a Maintenance Technician with the 2/51st Defense Battalion (Nike Hercules). In 1986, Norman became the Chief of the Maintenance Division, U.S. Army Engineer School, Fort Belvoir, Virginia. In 1992, he served as Senior Maintenance Advisor to the Commanding General, 1st Corps Support Command (COSCOM), Fort Bragg, North Carolina.

Mr. Norman retired in 1997 after 40 years of distinguished service to the U.S. Army and the Ordnance Corps.

Chief Warrant Officer Three Alvin Rose

Chief Warrant Officer Alvin Rose was inducted into the Hall of Fame in 2005.

Alvin Rose was born on June 24, 1944 in New Orleans, Louisiana. Rose entered the U.S. Army in 1962 serving as a personnel clerk in Alaska while reenlisting in 1964 to attend Explosive Ordnance Disposal (EOD) School.

In 1974, Mr. Rose was appointed a warrant officer and served as a project officer in the Doctrine and Training Literature Branch at the US Army Ordnance Missile and Munitions Center and School (USAOMMCS).

Mr. Rose retired from the military in 1984. In 1990, Rose accepted a position as Senior Management Analyst in the Weapons System Management Directorate, US Missile Command, Redstone Arsenal. Mr. Rose retired in 1999.

Chief Warrant Officer Five James A. Jackson

Chief Warrant Officer James A. Jackson was inducted into the Hall of Fame in 2014.

James A. Jackson was born in Greenback, Tennessee on January 21, 1946. In October 1964, he voluntarily enlisted in the US Army and completed Basic Training at Fort Gordon, Georgia. He was then assigned to the 504th Signal Company in Mannheim, Germany when he served as a field radio repairman.

In October 1980, Sergeant First Class Jackson received a direct appointment to Warrant Officer One as an Electronics Communications Technician and was assigned to the 327th Signal Battalion, Fort Bragg, North Carolina. Mr. Jackson culminated his career with his assignment to the 5th Signal Command's G4 Support Operations Division to support highly sensitive missions directed by the Joint Chiefs of Staff and the US Army Europe.

Mr. Jackson retired in 2008 after serving over 43 years of continuous active federal service. He is the longest serving 918E Communications and Electronics Maintenance Technician in the history of the Army.

Chief Warrant Officer Five Mickle C. Mitchell

Chief Warrant Officer Mickle C. Mitchell was inducted into the Hall of Fame in 2014.

Mickle C. Mitchell was born in Columbus, Georgia on August 8, 1951. He joined the Army in July 1970 through basic training at Fort Knox, Kentucky and Advanced Individual Training at Fort Rucker, Alabama. After serving as a helicopter mechanic, wheel mechanic, and senior maintenance sergeant, he became a Warrant Officer on February 3, 1986.

From 2002 until his retirement in 2007, Mr. Mitchell served as a Senior Training Developer at the Combined Arms Support Command (CASCOM) at Fort Lee, Virginia. As a member if the CASCOM, Mr. Mitchell developed and validated Programs of Instruction (POI) that trained over 2,500 officers, 15,000 Non-Commissioned Officers and 18,000 Enlisted Soldiers.

In recognition of his contributions to the Army, Mr. Mitchell was awarded the General Brehon B. Somervell Medal of Excellence.

Other African American Warrant Officers inducted into the Ordnance Corps Hall of Fame:

Chief Warrant Officer Five Harold L. DeBerry – inducted in 2010.

Chief Warrant Officer Five Harry L. Hobbs – inducted in 2013.

Chief Warrant Officer Five Ralph Williams, III – inducted in 2015.

The full citations for all Ordnance Corp Hall of Fame members can be found at: www.goordnance.army.mil/hof/hall_of_fame.html.

Honoring Those Who Served
Chief Warrant Officer Four (Retired)
Leonard A. Dungey
By Farrell J. Chiles, CW4, USA, Retired
(Originally Published in the USAWOA Newsliner - February 2017)

Leonard Alven Dungey is likely the oldest known Warrant Officer currently alive, having celebrated his 97th birthday on 19 August 2016. He served in the United States Army from 9 June 1941 to 30 June 30, a total of 20 years, 22 days.

Upon induction into the Army, Mr. Dungey was assigned to Camp Davis, North Carolina for basic training. As an enlisted man, he attained the rank of staff sergeant. Dungey was appointed a warrant officer on 21 December 1942 while assigned to the 99th Coast Artillery Regiment in Trinidad, British West Indies.

Mr. Dungey served in World War II. He deployed in September 1944 with the segregated (all Black) 597th Field Artillery Battalion, 92nd Infantry Division to Viareggio, Italy. Warrant Officer Junior Grade (WOJG) Dungey served as the battalion's personnel officer. At the height of World War II, there were 685 African American warrant officers in the Army. After the war and the downsizing of the force, as of May 31, 1946, only 89 African American warrant officers remained in the Continental United States and another 130 were Overseas. Mr. Dungey was retained on Active Duty. He received his last promotion (to CW4) on June 9, 1959. He retired from military service on June 30, 1961.

Mr. Dungey has remarkable memories of his military career. However, he seldom talks about that time in his life, since he shared his story with the world.

At the age of 95, in November 2014, Mr. Dungey authored a book, "The Best Man I Can Be: The Trials and Tribulations of a Black Chief Warrant Officer from World War II – The Astonishing Tale of One Man's Plight with American Racism". The book catalogs his experiences in the Army as an African American in both the segregated and integrated Army. The book is available at booksamillion.com; barnesandnoble.com; and amazon.com.

Chief Warrant Officer Dungey encountered racism throughout his military career.

While assigned as a reconnaissance officer for a searchlight battalion at Fort Stewart, Georgia, Mr. Dungey did not give up his seat reserved for white passengers and stand up on the bus. He was later reprimanded by the commanding general for his behavior. The general in essence said, "Go find yourself a good nigrah to show you how to act. If you lose your life down here, all the Army will do is ship your body back up north in a pine box". Mr. Dungey immediately put in a request for transfer to the Pentagon for combat duty. Sooner than later, he joined the 92nd Infantry Division at Fort Huachuca, Arizona.

In 1949, Mr. Dungey attended a six week officer's personnel management course at the Adjutant General School at Fort Lee, Virginia. He was the only black officer in the class. At the end of the course, the class president, a lieutenant colonel, informed Mr. Dungey that he could not attend the class graduation party at the officer's club because ladies from the outside would be in attendance.

At Fort Dix, New Jersey, Mr. Dungey was assigned as a personnel officer with the 9th Infantry Division, Army Basic Training. He was originally the Records Disposition Officer in the 'black" personnel section. Because of his successful results, the post adjutant general moved him to a larger section which included white soldiers. Mr. Dungey was later informed that the post commanding general ordered him back to the post's black service detachment because Mr. Dungey was a black warrant officer and could not be in charge of white troops. A few days later, Mr. Dungey drove to the Pentagon and requested a transfer. Less than a month later, he was headed to Germany.

Mr. Dungey received assignment orders for EUCOM (the European Command headquarters) in Heidelberg. He was further assigned to a trucking battalion stationed in Nuremberg. However, the lieutenant colonel in command of the battalion showed his racist and bigoted self. He had no intention of replacing the white lieutenant, in the position that was designated for a warrant officer, with a black warrant officer. Mr. Dungey was reassigned to a unit of his choice, a heavy-truck battalion in Frankfurt. He spent his entire three-year tour with that unit.

Mr. Dungey lives a quiet life with his wife, Virginia in Albion, Illinois. He makes a quarterly trip to the doctor in Evansville, Indiana, about an hour away. He has an office at home, a converted bedroom, which he uses as his getaway, since it's difficult for him to navigate the stairs to the basement, where his previous office was located. His office, surrounded by memorabilia, pictures, and artifacts of his life, is also where he listens to his LP album collection of jazz, swing music, and other music that reminds him of the 30's and 40's. He has an occasional glass of Johnnie Walker Black label (scotch). He spends most of the day watching television and observing birds outside his office window. Mr. Dungey stills stays in contact with a high school classmate who lives in St. Louis.

Words from a poem that Leonard Dungey wrote:
"Down the road, 'round the bend,
Black and proud to the end,
Dilemma ethnic, hateful shame.
Forget the hate, beware the blame.
For all that's just, that's true,
A patriot, through and through."

CW4 (Ret) Leonard Dungey   Leonard Dungey

*Mr. Dungey died on December 3, 2017.

Honoring Those Who Served
Chief Warrant Officer Five (Retired) Rufus N. Montgomery Sr.
Submitted by CW4 Farrell J. Chiles, USA, Ret.
(Originally published in the USAWOA Newsliner – February 2017)

Rufus N. Montgomery, Sr. was born on 6 October 1945 in Pensacola, Florida to Rufus and Mary Montgomery (both deceased). He had three sisters – Stella Reynolds, Nellie Lewis (deceased), and Lillie McReynolds (deceased). Montgomery began his military career as an enlisted soldier in 1965, serving his first tour of duty as a combat Infantryman and later as a cook with Company C, 1st Battalion, 503rd Airborne Infantry, 173rd Airborne Brigade (Separate), Bien Hoa, Vietnam. He rose to the rank of Sergeant First Class before his appointment as a warrant officer in 1977.

CW5 Montgomery performed to the highest levels of food services and was widely recognized as one of the foremost food service advisors in the Army. His assignments included the 36th Engineer Group (Combat Heavy), Fort Benning, Georgia and Operation Desert Shield/Desert Storm, Saudi Arabia; 1st Armored Division, Ansbach, Germany; US Army Natick Research and Development Laboratories, Natick, Massachusetts; 2nd Armored Cavalry Regiment, Nuremberg, Germany; 1st Battalion, 15th Field Artillery, 2nd Infantry Division, Camp Stanley, Korea; 2nd, 325th Airborne Infantry Battalion, 82nd Airborne Division, Fort Bragg, North Carolina; 2/509th Airborne/Mechanized Infantry, Mainz-Gonsenheim, Germany.

Mr. Montgomery's last assignment was as the Combined Arms Support Command Senior Personnel Proponency Officer, where he played an important role in the Army Training Leadership Development Panel Study on Army Transformation challenges and its effect on warrant officers in all grades. He is a member of the Quartermaster Hall of Fame, Class of 2007; a Distinguished Member of the Quartermaster Regiment; and was inducted as an Honorary Alumnus-Office of the Quartermaster General by the 44th Quartermaster General in June 1998. Montgomery served as a voting

(CASCOM) member of the original Warrant Officer Leader Development Council, officially established on January 4, 1999.

His military awards include the Legion of Merit, the Meritorious Service Medal (w/ Five Oak Leaf Clusters); the Army Achievement Medal (w/ four Oak Leaf Clusters); the Armed Forces Expeditionary Medal; the Vietnamese Cross of Gallantry with Palm; the Southwest Asia Service Medal; as well as the Saudi Arabia and Kuwait Liberation Medals. He also earned the Combat Infantryman Badge and Parachutist Badge.

Other significant accomplishments in CW5 Montgomery's military career include the first African American Chief Warrant Officer in the food service field to be selected to CW5 (selected below the zone in 1994); and the first African American Chief Warrant Officer to serve as the Senior Warrant Officer Advisor to the Commander, Combined Arms Support Command, Fort Lee, Virginia.

Mr. Montgomery's military career spanned nearly four decades, over 37 years. Since his retirement in 2003, he has continued to be active and productive in the military and Quartermaster communities, serving as a member of the Board of Directors of the United States Army Warrant Officer Association Scholarship Foundation (2003-2012) and as a current member of the Board of Advisors for the Quartermasters Foundation.

In July 2015, a corridor located within the Warrant Officer Technical College, Army Logistics University, was dedicated in his honor. On 14 April 2016, Mr. Montgomery was the recipient of the President's Lifetime Achievement Award, presented by Mrs. Dorothy McAuliffe, First Lady of the Commonwealth of Virginia and MG Darrell Williams, Commander, Combined Arms Support Command.

CW5 (Retired) Montgomery is currently serving as the 6th Honorary Chief Warrant Officer of the Quartermaster Regiment, Emeritus. He is the first African American to hold this position.

Rufus Montgomery and his wife Patricia have a daughter – Natalie Patrice Crawford (Kevin); two grandchildren, Patricia Iris, Kevin, Jr.; and son – Rufus N. Montgomery, Jr., a veteran of Operation Desert Shield/Desert Storm; a Combat Engineer who served with the 1st Armored Division, Saudi Arabia, based out of Ansbach, Germany.

CW5 (Ret) Montgomery serves as a deacon at the Pleasant Grove Baptist Church in Prince George, Virginia. He is an active participant in the NAACP, Prince George Virginia Branch, and a volunteer with the Association of Wounded Veterans in Petersburg, Virginia and a member of the Quartermaster Advisory Committee, Fort Lee, Virginia. Mr. Montgomery is enjoying life with his wife of 51 years and his family.

CW5 (Retired) Rufus N. Montgomery Sr.

Educational Achievements of African American Warrant Officers

By CW4 (Retired) Farrell J. Chiles
(Originally Published in the USAWOA Newsliner - February 2018)

In 2005, I wrote my first article on African American Warrant Officers. Since that time, I have written more than a dozen articles on African American Warrant Officers, many of which have appeared in the Newsliner.

For African American History Month 2018, I would like to share the profiles of several African American Warrant Officers who continued their civilian education and obtained doctorate degrees in their chosen educational fields. As always, if I missed someone, I extend my apologies.

Doris I. "Lucki" Allen – CW3 (Retired)

Ms. Allen received her Ph.D. in Psychology and Organizational Development from The Wright Institute in 1986. She is the author of "Three Days Past Yesterday – A Black Woman's Journey Through Incredibility". Ms. Allen is a member of the US Military Intelligence Corps Hall of Fame. The Warrant Officer Career College designated the Distinguished Honor Graduate Award in recognition of her service.

Georgene Davis-Dixon – CW5 (Retired)

Ms. Davis-Dixon received her Ph.D. in Organizational Psychology from Walden University in 2013. She is a 2014 inductee into the Quartermaster Distinguished Member of the Regiment (DMOR). Ms. Davis-Dixon is currently employed as a Veterans Affairs Human Resource Specialist at the VA Hospital in Fayetteville, North Carolina.

Ricky Godbolt – CW2 (Retired)

Mr. Godbolt received his Doctorate of Education (Ed.D.) in Education Leadership from the University of Phoenix in 2011. He served as the Director of the Center for Trades and Energy Training at Columbia Southern University in Waldorf, Maryland. Mr. Godbolt currently is the Apprenticeship and Training Representative at the United States Department of Labor in Washington DC.

Harry L. Hobbs – CW5 (Retired)

Mr. Hobbs received his Doctorate of Business Administration, Business Administration and Management, from The Florida Institute of Technology in 2017. He previously earned a Doctorate Degree in Human Resource Management from Pacific Western University in 1998. Mr. Hobbs was inducted into the Ordnance Hall of Fame in 2013. He currently is employed as the Site Director and Assistant Professor of Business at the Florida Institute of Technology in Huntsville, Alabama.

Lynda Smith – CW3 (Retired)

Ms. Smith received her Doctor of Education in Organizational Leadership from Argosy University in 2016. The topic of her dissertation was "A Qualitative Exploration of Barriers That Hinder Black American Women from Surpassing the Glass Ceiling Within the Federal Government". She served as the Executive Director for the Association of Pan African Doctoral Scholars. Ms. Smith is currently employed with the VA Loma Linda Healthcare System in San Bernardino County, California.

Fred Twitty – CW5 (Retired)

Mr. Twitty received his Ph.D. in Business, Homeland Security and Leadership Policy from Northcentral University in 2015. He is a Lifetime member in the Honor Society of Phi Kappa Phi. Mr. Twitty served as the Deputy Security Advisor, White House Military Office, the White House, during two separate Presidential Administrations. He is the former owner and Private Investigator of the Twitty Security Services Company

Cleveland Valrey – CW4 (Retired)

Mr. Valrey received his L.H.D., Litterarum Humaniorum (Doctor of Humanities) from Payne Bible College in Jackson, Mississippi. Mr. Valrey is the author of "Black Labor and Race – San Francisco Bay

Area in World War II". In 2001, he was inducted into the US Army Aviation Hall of Fame and in 2005 he was inducted into the US Army Ranger Hall of Fame. Currently, Mr. Valrey is a Worshipful Master at the Live Oak Masonic Lodge in Oakland, California.

James J. Williams – CW5

Mr. Williams is currently a candidate for a Ph.D. in Public Policy and Administration, Public Management and Leadership at Walden University. He is an adjunct professor with the University of Phoenix. Mr. Williams is a Senior Cyber Information Security Analyst at Northrop Grumman Corporation. Currently, he is on Active Duty with the United States Army - Joint Staff (Pentagon).

* * *

These African American Warrant Officers served the military and our country and continued to pursue opportunities outside of the military. Their commitment to achieving self-imposed educational goals serves as a challenge for others to follow.

During Black History Month 2018, please join me in saluting them and others who continue to set the example.

African American Warrant Officers' Biographies

Chief Warrant Officer Five Deshawn L. Bell

CW5 Deshawn L. Bell assumed duties as the Signal Regiment's fifth Regimental Chief Warrant Officer (RCWO) at Fort Gordon, GA on 16 September 2016. CW5 Bell previously served as the Command Chief Warrant Officer for the 311th Signal Command (Theater), Fort Shafter, Hawaii, August 2015 – August 2016. He was the Senior Network Operations Technician and was the primary technical advisor on all network and systems matters, especially as it related to strategic-to-tactical systems integration within US Army Pacific (USARPAC) Theater.

CW5 Bell proudly hails from Colorado Springs, Colorado. He is a 1987 graduate of Roy J. Wasson High School in Colorado Springs, CO. He entered the US Army in July 1988 as a Computer Programmer/Systems Analyst (MOS 74F). From 1989 – 1996, he served at Ft. Huachuca, Arizona; Pearl Harbor, Hawaii; and Alexandria, Virginia. He was selected to attend the Warrant Officer Candidate School in 1996, and was appointed a Warrant Officer One (WO1) in the Signal Corps.

After completing the Warrant Officer Basic Course at Ft. Gordon, he was stationed at Ft. Bragg in 1997 and served as the Automation Section OIC of the Corps Logistics Automation Office (CLAO) supporting the 1st Corps Support Command (Airborne).

In 2000, Mr. Bell was assigned to Fort Wainwright, Alaska where he served as the OIC of the Combat Service Support Automation Management Office (CSSAMO), supporting 172nd Infantry Brigade (Separate) and US Army Alaska (USARAK). In 2004, after attending the Warrant Officer Advanced Course, he was assigned to Ft. Lewis, Washington where he assumed duties as the I Corps G6 Data Network Planner, supporting I Corps' numerous operational missions throughout the Pacific. He attended the Warrant Officer Staff Course during this assignment. In 2007 he deployed to Camp Arifjan, Kuwait supporting the 335th Signal Command (Theater) and the US Army Central (ARCENT) Forward. He was further deployed to Kabul, Afghanistan and Camp Victory, Iraq as a Network Architecture Technician and later the Chief, Communications Engineering Branch supporting the Combined Security Transition Command-Afghanistan, and the Joint Network Communications Center - Iraq. After returning from deployment in 2008, CW5 Bell was assigned to US Army Pacific (USARPAC) and served as the USARPAC G6 Data Network Services Integrator and later the Senior IT Project Manager, Ft. Shafter, HI, supporting 311th Signal Command (Theater), USARPAC, and PACOM's numerous operational missions throughout the Pacific. He attended the Warrant Officer Senior Staff Course during this assignment.

CW5 Bell's prior assignment, October 2011 – July 2015, was serving as the Technical Director, Leader College of Network Operations (DoDIN), US Army Signal School, Cyber Center of Excellence, Ft. Gordon, GA. He was the senior technical advisor for all technical training provided to all Signal Officers, Warrant Officers, and NCO's on behalf of the Signal School and Cyber Center of Excellence.

His awards and decorations include the Legion of Merit, Bronze Star Medal, Meritorious Service Medal (5 OLC), Joint Service Commendation Medal, Army Commendation Medal (1 OLC), Joint Service Achievement Medal, Army Achievement Medal (4 OLC), Army Good Conduct Medal (2 awards), National Defense Service Medal (2 awards), Afghanistan Campaign Medal, Iraq Campaign Medal, Global War On Terrorism Expeditionary Medal, Global War on Terrorism Service Medal, NATO Medal, Parachutist Badge, the Joint Meritorious Unit Award, and the Bronze Order of Mercury.

CW5 Bell holds an Associate of Science Degree in Data Processing Technology from Hawaii Pacific University, a Bachelor of

Science Degree in Computer and Information Sciences from University of Maryland University College, a Master of Science Degree in Information Technology Management from Touro University International, and a graduate of all required Professional Military Education. Additionally, CW5 Bell is a Project Management Professional (PMP), and a Certified Information Systems Security Professional (CISSP).

CW5 Deshawn L. Bell is married to the former Susan A. Nantz of Titusville, Florida.

He and his spouse have a blended family of seven daughters -- all adults and out of the house pursuing their dreams.

Chief Warrant Officer Three Carlos A. Bianco Jr.

I was born in New London, Connecticut on December 10, 1973. My parents, Carlos Blanco Sr. and Velneeta Darnell, are both military veterans. My father was in the Marine Corps and served in Vietnam; my mother served in the United States Army Reserve. Although my parents divorced shortly after my first birthday, my childhood was one of structure and discipline. Until the age of 12, I was primarily raised by my mother and grandmother. I lived with my father and grandmother through my high school years. In 1992, I graduated from T.C. Williams High School (Remember the Titans), Alexandria, Virginia.

My military career began February 27, 1991. I joined the Connecticut Army National Guard at age 17 during my junior year of high school. Throughout the summer of 1991, I attended Basic Training at Fort Jackson, SC. Shortly after returning from my IET, I completed an inter-state transfer to the Virginia Army National Guard (VAARNG). I was assigned to A Co, 1/170, 2nd Bde, 29th ID. In 1992, after graduation, I completed 71L Advanced Individual Training (AIT) and was reassigned to HQs, 1/170, 2nd Bde, 29th ID. While assigned to the 1/170th I served as an S1 Administrative Clerk and S3 Administrative Clerk.

In 1995, I received a Title 10 AGR tour and was assigned to the Fort Bragg Operational Support Airlift Detachment, Fort Bragg, North Carolina. During my 3 year tour at Fort Bragg, I served as the Detachment Administrative NCO, and Detachment NCOIC. I completed PLDC, was promoted to Sergeant, and reclassified to 93P (Aviation Operations). In 1998, I was reassigned to the Panama Regional Flight Detachment, Howard AFB, Panama. While assigned to the Panama Regional Flight Detachment, I served as an Aviation

Operations NCO and deployed to Soto Cano AB, Honduras in support of the Hurricane Mitch Relief Effort.

In 1999, upon completion of my tour in Panama, I was assigned to the United Transportation Command, Scott AFB, Illinois. While assigned to USTRANSCOM, I served as a Joint Airlift Scheduler, completed both BNCOC and ANCOC, and received promotions to Staff Sergeant and Sergeant First Class. In 2002, I was reassigned to the Operational Support Airlift Agency (OSAA), Fort Belvoir, VA. While assigned to OSAA, I completed two deployments to Kuwait, held multiple leadership positions, was promoted to Master Sergeant, and finished undergraduate school.

In 2005, I attended Warrant Officer Candidate School, was appointed to WO1 and reassigned to ARNG G1, National Guard Bureau (NGB), Arlington, Virginia. While assigned to NGB, I served as a DEERS/RAPIDS Project Manager and completed the 42OAWarrant Officer Basic Course. In 2007, I resigned my Title 10 AGR Tour, inter-state transferred to the Pennsylvania Army National Guard (PAARNG), and accepted a Title-32 AGR assignment as S1, Eastern ARNG Aviation Training Site (EAATS), Fort Indiantown Gap, Pennsylvania. While assigned to EAATS, I was promoted to CW2, completed the ARNG Bn/Bde S1 Course and Warrant Officer Advanced Course.

In 2010, I volunteered for an assignment with the 166th Regiment, Regional Training Institute, Fort Indiantown Gap, Pennsylvania, to become a Warrant Officer Candidate School (WOCS) Training, Advising, and Counseling (TAC) Officer. I had multiple responsibilities which included TAC Officer and Course Manager for both Officer Candidate and Warrant Officer Candidate Schools.

In 2014, I was reassigned to my current position as the S1 / Adjutant for the 166th Regiment, Regional Training Institute. Although assigned as the S1 / Adjutant, I maintain my certification and involvement as a WOCS TAC Officer. In 2015 I attended Warrant Officer Intermediate Level Education.

My awards include the Meritorious Service Medal (2OLC), Joint Service Commendation Medal, Army Commendation Medal (SOLC), Joint Service Achievement Medal (1OLC), Army Achievement Medal

(4OLC), Good Conduct Medal (3rd Award), Army Component Achievement Medal, National Defense Service Medal (Bronze Star), Global War on Terrorism Expeditionary Medal, Global War on Terrorism Service Medal, Armed Forces Reserve Medal (M Device), Non-Commissioned Officer Professional Development Ribbon (3rd Award), Army Service Ribbon, Overseas Service Ribbon, Joint Meritorious Unit Award, Aircraft Crewmember Badge, Army Staff Identification Badge, and German Armed Forces Proficiency Badge.

I am married to the former CaSeal Davis of Las Vegas, Nevada. We have two sons and two daughters, Michael (24), Anthony (21), Lalasa (10), and Elaynee (5). My family and I reside in Harrisburg, PA. My hobbies include quality time with my family, music and physical fitness.

Chief Warrant Officer Five Lawrence Blackwell

Chief Warrant Officer Five Lawrence Blackwell was born on May 20, 1961 in Brodnax, Virginia, and joined the Army in 1979. After eleven years as an enlisted and Noncommissioned Officer, he was appointed a Warrant Officer in 1990 and began his 21-year career in the Warrant Officer ranks with multiple deployments overseas in support of the contingency operations.

From 2006 through 2008, CW5 Blackwell was attached to the 1st Armor Division during Operation Iraqi Freedom and supported over 2,000 tracked and wheeled vehicles organized for combat operations. He directly contributed to the 97% operations readiness rate for the Brigade Combat Team while deployed in a combat zone. His efforts enabled units to conduct over 300 combat, logistical patrols, traveling over 76,000 mile.

CW5 Blackwell culminated his career in 2009 as he provided timely logistics support and leadership to the 1st Cavalry Division in a deployment with over 3,000 pieces of equipment. He coordinated and synchronized the efforts of the Defense Logistics Agency, U.S. Army Tank-Automotive and Armaments Command, and the Joint Munitions Command in support of a Brigade Combat Team deployed to Iraq. He coordinated the 402nd Army Field Support Brigade Mobile Retrograde Property Assistance Team to receive, process, and retrograde over 600 vehicles and 1,000 pieces of class VII rolling stock. Upon return from Operation Iraqi Freedom, CW5 Blackwell monitored and synchronized the repair and return of over 26,000 individual pieces of equipment through the Army Sustainment Command RESET program.

Chief Warrant Officer Five Blackwell retired in 2011.

Chief Warrant Officer Three Alex Blain

CW3 Alex Blain entered active duty in July 2000 from the state of Massachusetts and in September 2007, CW3 Blain commissioned as an Ordnance Warrant Officer from the Warrant Officer Career College (WOCC) at Fort Rucker, Alabama.

CW3 Blain's duty assignments include 203rd Brigade Support Battalion, 3rd Armored Brigade Combat Team, 3rd Infantry Division, Fort Benning, Georgia; 725th Brigade Support Battalion (Airborne), 4th Brigade Combat Team (Airborne), 25th Infantry Division, Joint Base Elmendorf-Richardson, Alaska; Distribution Management Center (DMC), U.S. Army Sustainment Command, Rock Island Arsenal, Illinois; Training with Industry (TWI), Lockheed Martin Missiles & Fire Control, Camden, Arkansas; Combined Arms Support Command (CASCOM), Fort Lee, VA. CW3 Blain has deployed three times to Iraq and twice to Afghanistan.

CW3 Blain's military education includes WOCS), WOBC, WOAC, WOILE, Action Officer Development Course, Contracting Officer Representative Course (COR), Support Operation Course Phase I & II, Demonstrated Master Logistician, Joint Logistics Course, Capabilities Development Course, Airborne School, Jumpmaster School, Air Assault School, and Pathfinder School.

His awards and decorations include the Bronze Star Medal (OLC), Meritorious Service Medal (3OLC), Army Commendation Medal (3OLC), Army Achievement Medal, Army Good Conduct Medal (#2), National Defense Service Medal, Afghanistan Campaign Medal (2 Campaign Bronze Stars), Iraqi Campaign Medal (3 Campaign Bronze Stars), Global War on Terror Expeditionary Medal, Global War on Terror Service Medal, Military Outstanding Volunteer Service Medal,

NCO Professional Development Ribbon, Army Service Ribbon, Overseas Service Ribbon (#4), Valorous Unit Award, and the Meritorious Unit Award (2OLC). He also earned the Combat Action Badge, Master Parachutist Badge, Air Assault Badge, Pathfinder Badge, as well as Chilean Jump Wings, Canadian Jump Wings, Australian Jump Wings, and Royal Thai Jump Wings. He is a recipient of the Ordnance Order of Samuel Sharpe.

CW3 Blain received his Associates of Arts in General Studies from the University of Phoenix, Arizona and Bachelor of Science in Business Administration from Columbia College, Missouri, and Master of Science in Management (Leadership Concentration) from Troy University, Alabama.

Warrant Officer One Mari Blanding's Autobiography
(Submitted as a Warrant Officer Candidate)

My name is Mari McKinzie Blanding. I was born a twin on September 22, 1973 in Saigon, Vietnam. Unfortunately my twin brother was stillborn. My father at the time was enlisted in the United States Army as a 57F, Graves Registration and my mother worked as a seamstress. My parents married and moved to Thailand in 1975 and in 1976 we were stationed at Fort Bliss in El Paso, Texas where my younger sister Jacqueline was born. Being associated with the military, my family and I have had our fair share of permanent change of stations, included were: Fort Hood, TX; Frankfurt, Germany; Fort Bragg, North Carolina and finally Hawaii. My parents decided to make a permanent home in Fayetteville, NC where my sister and I could have better stability; remaining in the same school district was priority. After a couple of years my parents divorced due to the stress of separation of having one parent holding down the household while the other had a military obligation to fulfill. I attended the majority of my education at the Cumberland County school systems and as soon as I graduated from high school in 1992, I enlisted in the United States Army under the Delayed Entry Program.

My first duty station was Kitzingen, Germany where I worked as a 92A, Automated Logistics Specialist. I was also stationed at Fort Stewart, Georgia; Fort Bragg, NC; deployed to Camp Caldwell, Iraq with the North Carolina National Guard and I recently came back from a deployment with Alpha Company 351st Aviation Support Battalion at Camp Buehring, Afghanistan. I began my career as a 92Y, Unit Supply Sergeant in July 2009 with Detachment 1, Alpha Company 351st Aviation Support Battalion out of Cheraw, South Carolina. On

April 1, 2016, I was promoted to Sergeant First Class and assigned to Joint Force Headquarters where I am an inspector on the Maintenance Assistance and Instruction Team while on M-day status. As a technician, I am the GCSS-Army Administrator for the USPFO for South Carolina.

I am currently enrolled in online college courses with Columbia Southern University and will graduate with an Associates of Science in Business Administration in February of next year. My goal is to continue furthering my education with plans on receiving a Bachelor degree in the same major. I am married to another service member in the South Carolina National Guard, SSG Walter Blanding; he is currently the Battalion S4 for HSC 351st Aviation Support Battalion and I must say does an excellent job of it and he knows supply like the back of his hand.

We married on April 13, 2013 at the Sumter's Opera House and if you ever get the chance to visit my office at the USPFO (SSA Section) you will see the many family wedding photos and corky little gadgets all over my office including my samurai sword. So yes, you can say that I am quite the proud wife! We are also proud parents to our daughters, Angela (23 years of age) and Zasha (17 years of age). Angela is his daughter from a previous relationship and Zasha is my daughter from my first marriage. Angela is married to a service member in the Navy and is currently pursuing a degree in design and Zasha who has been an honor roll student since the seventh grade and currently holds a GPA of 3.6 desires to attend a four year college here in South Carolina next year.

For my pastime, I enjoy fishing. All I need is some fishing line and hooks and I can rig up just about anything and I can assure you that I will bring home some fish by the end of the day. As I sit here and ponder to myself, I remember my parents always reminding me, "with hard work comes great reward," and that is what I base a lot of my achievements off of. I recently got promoted to Sergeant First Class and it was one of my proudest accomplishments because I earned that #1 spot on the promotion list through hard work and determination but now I can say, I feel I have maximized my career potential as a non-commissioned officer. I want to approach a different avenue so I can open up more opportunities, challenge myself, and gain new knowledge to mentor fellow soldiers and of course to make my family proud!

As for my immediate family, the young man that was once a 57F is currently a retired SGM and a radiologist in San Antonio, Texas. That young girl, who was once a seamstress making little to nothing, now owns her own business as a manicurist and my younger sister Jacqueline, is a clinic manager in Fayetteville, NC and also holds a degree in radiology. As for me, I cannot wait till my parents witness my Warrant Officer Candidate Pinning Ceremony and see me complete my ultimate goals in my career!

MARI M. BLANDING
WOC, USA
Class 17-001

Update: Ms. Blanding is the "first" African American female Property Book (920) Warrant Officer in the South Carolina Army National Guard.

Chief Warrant Officer Four Phillip Maxie Brashear

Phillip Brashear is the son of Carl and Junetta Brashear and was born in Honolulu, Hawaii on July 3, 1962, exactly 11 months to the day of former President, Barak Obama. He is also 1980 graduate from I.C. Norcom High School in Portsmouth, Virgina. Upon graduation from high school, he was given a scholarship to wrestle at Old Dominion University in Norfolk, Va. where he competed for one year. In Sep 1981, he began his military career by joining the Naval Reserves as a Jet Engine Mechanic at Naval Squadron VAW-78; an E-2C Hawkeye unit at the Naval Air Station in Norfolk, Va.

In July 1983, he began his civilian occupation as a government employee at the Norfolk Naval Shipyard in Portsmouth, Va., as an Electrician Helper. In May 1989, he graduated from the NADEP Apprentice program as an Electronic Mechanic. Later that same year, Phillip left the Naval Reserves and joined the Virginia Army National Guard in Richmond, Va. In January of 1990, he was appointed a Warrant Officer Candidate and was sent to Army Flight training at Ft Rucker, Alabama in June of 1990. He completed Initial Rotary Wing Training and became a Warrant Officer Pilot in the Army in June of 1991. In April of 1994, Phillip left his competitive civil job at NADEP and became a Virginia Army National Technician for the Army National Guard at the Army Aviation Support Facility located at the Richmond International Airport. In April of 2002, Phillip returned to competitive civil service employment with the Defense Logistics Agency as a Quality Specialist at the Defense Supply Center, in Richmond, Va.

In November of 2005, Phillip was deployed to Iraq with his Army National Guard unit and returned in February 2007. He retired from the Army National Guard in November 2007. In May of 2009, Phillip returned to the military by joining the Army Reserves as a Rear Detachment Commander for Bravo and Delta Companies of the 5-159th General Support Aviation Battalion located at Ft Eustis, Virginia. Phillip also served as the 5-159th GSAB as the Battalion Maintenance Officer and currently as the Battalion Public Affairs Officer.

In November of 2013, Phillip joined the local Civil Air Patrol unit, located at the Chesterfield Airport at the rank of Major. As a civilian, Phillip is a Weapon System Support Manager for the Air Force for the Defense Logistics Agency.

Phillip is married to Sandra Brashear who is a retired (Army active duty / Army National Guard / Army Reservist) and current employee for the Virginia Department of Social Services. They reside in Sandston, Va. with their 16 year-old, son Tyler, (also a junior member of the Civil Air Patrol)

Note:

Phillip is the third son of the late Master Chief, Master Diver Carl Brashear, the subject of the Hollywood movie, 'Men of Honor'. Through his father's legendary American Military Hero status, Phillip has had the opportunity to share his dad's story on numerous occasions ranging from the staff at the White House and the Pentagon, various military organizations, church functions, museums, youth groups, and various local civic organizations. Phillip has also travelled internationally to represent his famous father. Phillip has represented the Army as well at events like the Essence Music Festival, college and university events, church organizations, and various civic and youth groups for his own extraordinary career as a helicopter pilot.

Featured Speeches and appearances:

Feb 22, 2015 – 80th Army Training Command, Richmond, Va.
https://www.army.mil/article/143278/Son_of_honor

Oct 1, 2015 – White House Communication Staff, Washington D.C.
http://www.carlbrashear.org/eventsarticles2015.html#whv

Feb 21, 2016 – Beulah Baptist Church, Rixeyville, Va.
http://www.dailyprogress.com/starexponent/dare-to-dream---son-speaks-about-navy-s/article_db830dd0-d8ee-11e5-b6eb-5f52bfc348cd.html

Feb 25, 2016 – Military Sealift Command, Norfolk, Va.
http://www.navy.mil/submit/display.asp?story_id=93281

Mar 3, 2016 – Army Aviation Association of America Feature Article
http://www.carlbrashear.org/eventsarticles2016.html#cos

Mar 9, 2016 – Powhatan Middle School, Powhatan, Va.
https://issuu.com/powhatantoday/docs/20160309rspa/1

Mar 23, 2016 - Watch Ambassador for the Oris Watch Company Basel, Switzerland
https://www.youtube.com/watch?v=YIGYm02LzX8

Apr 3, 2016 – Disciples of Men Retreat, Wakefield, Va.
http://www.ccinva.org/wp-content/uploads/2011/12/DM-Registration-2016.pdf

Chief Warrant Officer Five Jerome L. Bussey
United States Army Engineer School Regimental Chief Warrant Officer

CW5 Jerome Bussey is currently the fourth Regimental Chief Warrant Officer. He completed the Warrant Officer Candidate School and Engineer Warrant Officer Basic Course in 1999. CW5 Bussey served as the Utilities Operations and Maintenance Technician with the 14th Field Hospital, Fort Benning, Georgia; as the Utilities Operations and Maintenance Technician for the 67th Combat Support Hospital, Wuerzburg, Germany; as the Commander of the 72nd Survey and Design Detachment, Fort Knox, Kentucky; as the Engineer, Military Police, and Chemical Warrant Officer Assignment Officer, Human Resource Center of Excellent, Fort Knox, Kentucky; as the Facility Manager in Polices, Plans and Requirements Directorate, White House and as the Personnel Policy Integrator, Active Army, Warrant Officer Promotions, HQDA G1, Pentagon. His combat tours include serving as the Utilities Operations and Maintenance Technician for the 67th Combat Support Battalion in Iraq and as the Commander for the 72nd Survey and Design Detachment in Iraq.

His awards and decorations include the Bronze Star Medal, Defense Meritorious Service Medal, Meritorious Service Medal (4OLCs), Army Commendation Medal (4OLCs), Army Achievement Medal (5OLCs), Army Good Conduct Medal (4th Award); National Defense Service Medal (2ND Award), Noncommissioned Officer Professional Development Service Ribbon, Army Service Ribbon and Overseas Ribbon with numeral five. He is also authorized to wear the Presidential Support and Army Staff Badge.

CW5 Bussey's professional military education includes the Engineer Warrant Officer Basic Course and the Engineer Warrant Officer Advance Course (Fort Leonard Wood, MO); Warrant Officer Intermediate Level Education and Warrant Officer Senior Service College (Fort Rucker, AL); Joint Engineering Officer Course (Fort Leonard Wood, MO); How the Army Runs, Army Force Management School (Fort Belvoir, VA) and Senior Leader Seminar, Army War College's Center for Strategic Leadership (Shepherdstown, WV). He has a MBA with an emphasis in Project Management and has his Project Management Professional and Facility Management Professional certifications.

He is married to Sharon, has three sons and four grandchildren.

Chief Warrant Officer Three Christina Carter

Chief Warrant Officer Three Christina Carter is a native of Alabama. She enlisted in the Army National Guard as an E4 Personnel Information Systems Management Specialist (75F) in January 1998 completing basic and advanced individual training at Fort Jackson, South Carolina. She began her fulltime career in the military while in the enlisted ranks in 2001 as a Personnel Services Clerk with continued advancements as an Initial Active Duty Training (IADT) Manager, the State Personnel Security Manager, and Budget Analyst.

Then "Sergeant Carter", motivation continued by completing Warrant Officer Candidate School receiving her appointment as a Warrant Officer One in September 2009. She went on to complete the Adjutant General's Warrant Officer Basic and Advance courses obtaining her current rank as Chief Warrant Officer Three. She earned a Bachelor of Science Degree in Management of Human Resources from Faulkner University and a Master's Degree in Occupational Safety and Health from Columbia Southern University. She is currently the S1 Chief, Human Resources Technician at the 31st Chemical Brigade, Tuscaloosa.

CW3 Carter deployments include Operation Enduring Freedom, Ft. Benning, Georgia 2003 and Operation Iraqi Freedom, Camp Beuring, Kuwait 2004-2005.

Her awards and decorations include the Meritorious Service Medal, Army Commendation Medal (2OLC), Army Achievement Medal (3OLC), Army Good Conduct Medal, Army Reserve Components Achievement Medal (3OLC), National Defense Service medal (2nd award), Army Service Ribbon, Overseas Service Ribbon, Armed Forces Reserve Medal with "M" Device (2nd award), Global

War on Terrorism Expeditionary Medal and the Global War on Terrorism Service Medal.

Chief Warrant Officer Five Terry D. Clark

Chief Warrant Officer Five Terry D. Clark or "TDC" was born in Humboldt, Tennessee. He began his U.S. Army career in July 1990. He completed basic training at Fort Jackson, South Carolina and AIT at Fort Gordon, GA as a Signal Corps Radio Repairman (MOS 29E). From 1990-1997, he served at Schofield Barracks, Hawaii; Fort Gordon, Georgia; Vilseck, Germany and deployed to Hungary and Bosnia-Herzegovina in support of Operations Joint Guard & Endeavor with the 1st Infantry Division.

In 1997, he was selected as an Ordnance Electronic Systems Maintenance Warrant Officer (MOS 948B), and completed all initial Warrant Officer training. From 1997 to 2002, Mr. Clark served his first assignment as the Battalion Signal Maintenance Officer for the 51st Signal Battalion (ABN), 35th Signal Brigade (ABN) at Fort Bragg, North Carolina. From 2002 to 2003, he served as the Avionics Maintenance Officer & Platoon Leader for the 602nd Aviation Support Battalion, 2nd Infantry Division, Camp Stanley, Korea. From 2003 to 2005, he served as the C&E and Intelligence Electronics Warfare Maintenance Officer for the 125th Military Intelligence Battalion, 25th Infantry Division (Light), Schofield Barracks, Hawaii including a deployment to Operation Enduring Freedom-Afghanistan.

From 2005 to 2006, he was selected as the Division C4ISR Installation Facility OIC to oversee digital system installations and modularity transformation activities for the entire 25th Infantry Division. From 2006 to 2010, he served as the Brigade Signal Officer, Maintenance Control Officer and Brigade Communications and Electronics Maintenance Officer the 402nd BSB, 5th Stryker Brigade

Combat Team, Fort Lewis, Washington including the 1st SBCT to support combat operations in OEF-Afghanistan.

From 2010 to 2014, Mr. Clark served as an Integrated Logistics Supportability Capability Developer for the Combined Arms Support Command SCoE, Fort Lee, Virginia. From 2014 to 2016, he served as the Theater Electronic Systems Maintenance Advisor for the 21st Theater Sustainment Command, Kaiserslautern, Germany. Mr. Clark is currently serving as the Warrant Officer Division Chief (CMF 948B/D) for the Ordnance Electronic Maintenance Training Department, U.S. Army Ordnance School at Fort Gordon, Georgia.

CW5 Clark holds a Master of Science in Human Resources and Graduate Certificate in Organizational Leadership from Chapman University; Bachelor Science in Business Administration from Hawaii Pacific University; Associate of Arts in Management from Georgia Military College. He was awarded the Demonstrated Master Logistician designation by the International Society of Logistics.

He is a graduate of all Warrant Officer Professional Military Education to include Lean Six Sigma-Black Belt, Manpower and Force Management, Joint Logistics, Capabilities Developer, Support Operations, Basic Instructor, Training Developer, Senior Training and Education Manager and numerous other courses.

His military awards and decorations include the Legion of Merit Medal; Bronze Star Medal; Meritorious Service Medal (3 OLC); Army Commendation Medal (3 OLC); Army Achievement Medal (1 OLC); a Meritorious Unit Citation; Air Assault and Driver's Badges. He is the recipient of the Ordnance Corps Regimental Order of Samuel Sharpe and the Signal Corps Regimental Bronze Order of Mercury.

CW5 Clark and his wife, Wanda, of Philadelphia, PA have two daughters.

Chief Warrant Officer Five Alston Cleary

Chief Warrant Officer Five (CW5) Alston Cleary is a native of Jamaica. He entered the military on 17 May 1988. He attended basic and advanced individual training at Fort Leonard Wood, Missouri and then went on to airborne school in Fort Benning, Georgia. As an enlisted Soldier he served in the 37th Engineer Battalion and the 82nd Airborne Division at Ft Bragg, NC and also in Korea.

CW5 Cleary was selected as a Warrant Officer candidate and attended the Warrant Officer Candidate course in June 1996; he was appointed a Warrant Officer One on 2 August 1996. His assignments as a Warrant Officer that followed were 567th Transportation Company at Fort Eustis, Virginia where he spent 33 months before again being assigned to the 520th Maintenance Company in Korea. His next assignment took him to Fort Hood, Texas where he was assigned from January 2001 until October 2009. While at Fort Hood, Mr. Cleary served in the 62nd Engineer Combat Battalion units: 74th Multi-Role Bridge Company (Assault Float Bridge), 68th Combat Support Equipment (Heavy), and Headquarters and Headquarters Company 62nd Engineer Battalion as the battalion maintenance technician.

While at Fort Hood, CW5 Cleary deployed to Iraq in 2003, and again in 2005 for 14 months, and Afghanistan in 2008 for 15 months. CW5 Cleary was then reassigned to the 82nd Sustainment Brigade, Fort Bragg, North Carolina in October 2009 where he served for 29 months in the support operations maintenance readiness branch before again being reassigned in April 2012 to the G-4 staff, 1st Sustainment Command (Theater) at Fort Bragg, North Carolina. CW5 Cleary was then reassigned to Fort Wainwright, AK where he served as the deputy director of the Logistics Readiness Center from 29 January 2014 until

3 February 2017. CW5 Cleary is currently assigned as the Senior Ordnance Ground Maintenance Warrant Officer in the G4 of the U.S. Army Sustainment Command at Rock Island Arsenal, IL.

CW5 Cleary holds a Master's degree in Business Administration with a concentration in Logistics from Touro University. He also was inducted into the International Society of Logistics and was awarded the designation of Demonstrated Master Logistician. He also holds a six sigma black belt certification from Touro University.

Mr. Cleary's military education includes the Engineer Equipment Repair Technician basic and advanced course, Warrant Officer Staff and senior staff course.

His awards and decorations include the Bronze Star Medal, Meritorious Service Medal with four oak leaf clusters, Army Commendation Medal with four oak leaf clusters, Army Achievement Medal with silver leaf, Army Good Conduct Medal with two bronze loops, National Defense Service Medal with bronze star, Afghanistan Campaign Medal with one campaign star, Iraq Campaign Medal with four campaign stars, Global War on Terrorism Expeditionary and Service medals, Korea Defense Service Medal, Overseas Ribbon with numeral five, NATO medal, Driver and Mechanic Badge, Honduras parachutist badge, and Senior Parachutist Badge. CW5 Cleary was awarded the Ordnance Order of Samuel Sharpe and the Bronze de Fleury medal.

CW5 Cleary is married to Angella and together there are five children; Fayann, Kirk, Eldon, Davon, and Aldith. They have six grandchildren; Tatyana, Zah'Kira, Kavel, Kezra, Summer, and Kayla.

Chief Warrant Officer Two Amber L. Coleman-Allsup

Chief Warrant Officer (CW2) Amber L. Coleman-Allsup serves as a fulltime Chief Warrant Officer for the Pennsylvania Army National Guard.

CW2 Amber L. Coleman-Allsup, 34, born 12 January 1984. Born in Hershey Pa, and raised through childhood in Carlisle Pa of mother Judie A. Shealer-Peterson, father Ronald J. Coleman, and step-mother Vivian A. Coleman. She married her husband, Blake E. Allsup on 29 June 2008. Together they have four children, Adazhay A. Allsup, Adomani A. Allsup, Adamiya A. Allsup, and Adonijah A. Allsup.

Assigned to the 2nd Battalion, 166th Regiment, CW2 Allsup serves a WOCS Chief Instructor and TAC Officer for the Officer Candidate School (OCS), Warrant Officer Candidate School (WOCS), and Pre-Warrant Officer Candidate Course (PWOCC).

On a fulltime basis, CW2 Allsup serves as a Federal 920B Supply Systems Technician. By holding the position of supervisor at the Unit Equipment Training Site (UTES) located at Fort Indiantown Gap (FIG), PA, CW2 Allsup offers her expertise in logistics to accommodate the training of Army units across the United States.

CW2 Allsup enlisted into the military on 3 October 2001. At the age of seventeen and only days after the horrific September 11th 2001 terrorist attacks on the United States, CW2 Allsup made the conscious decision that her mission in life was to protect those she loved by building a career in the armed forces. After graduating from Carlisle High School, Class of 2002, CW2 Allsup left for Basic Combat Training (BCT) at Fort Jackson, South Carolina. Advancing on to her Advanced Individual Training (AIT) she progressed to the Quartermaster School at Fort Lee, Virginia in the winter of 2002. In

2014 CW2 made the conscious decision to further her career by becoming a Warrant Officer for the United States Army. She graduated from Fort Rucker, Alabama on 29 May 2014, appointed as a new Quartermaster Warrant Officer in the Warrant Officer Cohort.

For the past 16 years CW2 Allsup has devoted her profession to the armed forces, being awarded an array of Army medals for unprecedented performance and accomplishments. CW2 Allsup was nominated as the Warrant Officer of the Year in 2015 for her outstanding performance. CW2 Allsup is Master Fitness Trainer Certified. She has received multiple Army Achievement Medals, Army Reserve Component Achievement Medals, National Defense Service Medal, Armed Forces Reserve Army Medal, to include, being awarded the Army Reserve Component Overseas Training Medal in 2005 for outstanding performance while attending training in Grafenwöhr, Germany. She has also obtained numerous Army Physical Fitness awards from various trainings and competitions.

Alongside her fulltime military career, CW2 Allsup serves as the Treasurer of the Warrant Officer Association, Keystone Chapter of Pennsylvania. She is a fulltime student at the University of Phoenix pursuing a Master's Degree in Business Accounting. Alongside her 10 year old son, Adomani Allsup, a co-founder of "Operation Recognition" in Steelton, PA, CW2 Allsup assists with recognizes veterans and their families by presenting such heroes with their high school diplomas they never received due to being called to war. She is the founder and owner of her own personal fitness program, "Fit Parents First" that she offers to local school districts to bring parents and their children together through fitness.

CW2 Allsup is also the officer mentor for the "Female to Female Mentorship Program" of the Army Reserve Regional Training Site at FIG. She continues to stay actively engaged in her community, competes in marathons, half marathons, various races and fitness challenges, all while continuously working to advance in all that she does.

Chief Warrant Officer Two Corey Alan Copeland

My name is Corey Alan Copeland. I was brought into this world in Reading, Pennsylvania, Sunday, 12 July 1981, at 2102. I have been a proud lifelong resident of Reading, PA ever since.

My parents, Cleve and Lois Copeland, have been married for 35 years. They encouraged me at an early age to find joy in something and turn that joy into a career. Since the age 12, I found that joy; it was computers. Since that time, I have become extremely versatile in several aspects of Information Technology. My skillset was in high demand my senior year of high school, which prompted a Recruiter from the Pennsylvania Army National Guard to come knocking on my door. Next thing I knew, I was sworn in at MEPs on 22 April 1999.

I have continued to serve my country and the commonwealth of PA since that time.

During my 18+ years of service, I had the full support of my high school sweetheart and wife Mrs. Toshira Copeland. She and I made this journey together and along the way created to perfect little people of our own, Camden (6) Averie (3). While my family has always been my priority, the Warrant Officer Corps is a very close second. I made the decision to become part of the elite in February 2009. Not only have I enjoyed serving as a technical expert, I have devoted myself to mentoring up and coming Warrants and becoming a TAC officer.

Associates Degree Berks Technical Institute, May 2003
Bachelor's Degree (Magna Cum Laude), November 2013
Warrant Officer One, 27 February 2009
Assistant TAC Officer from 2009 – 2014

Chief Warrant Officer Five (Retired) Leslie Errol Cornwall

CW5 Cornwall faithfully served our Army for over 35 years upon his retirement. Throughout his career, he distinguished himself through exceptionally meritorious service and served as an example that all Soldiers should strive to emulate.

CW5 Cornwall's illustrious career began in the United States Virgin Islands, in 1977, when he enlisted in the Army. After attaining the rank of E-7, he was selected to become a Warrant Officer in 1992 and served another 20 years for his country.

From 1977 - 1979 Senior Tactical Circuit Controller, B Co 142nd Signal Battalion, 2nd Armored Division, Fort Hood, TX. From 1979 - 1981 Team Chief Multichannel Radio Site, HHB 38th ADA Brigade, Osan AFB, Korea. From 1981 - 1981 Circuit Control Section SGT, A Co 122nd Signal Battalion, 2nd Infantry Division (M), Camp Casey, Korea. From 1981 - 1982, Circuit Control Section SGT, C Co 304th Signal Battalion, 1st Signal Brigade, Camp Colbern, Korea. From 1982 - 1984, Multichannel Equipment Section SGT, C Co 54th Signal Battalion, 3rd Signal Brigade, Fort Hood, TX. From 1984 - 1987, TRI-TAC System Planner, HHC 72nd Signal Battalion, he was also involved heavily within the Family Readiness Support Group. From 1987 - 1988, Multichannel Equipment Planner, HHC 304th Signal Battalion, Camp Colbern, Korea. From 1988 - 1991, he was the Senior Instructor/Writer for TRI-TAC for WOAC, WOBC, ASI-K7, F39 and F35 Courses. From 1991 - 1992, he was selected above his peers to become the platoon sergeant of a Mobile Subscriber Equipment (MSE) Area Platoon, 258th Signal Co (FORSCOM), Fort Gordon, GA.

His leadership and technical skills allowed for a very successful conversion of a cable construction company to an MSE area Signal company. From 1992 - 1995, he became the Network Management Technician, 3rd Signal Brigade, Fort Hood, TX. He introduced High Speed Data Networks to III Corps, and also upgraded MSE switches to ESOP and ATM capabilities improving the communications of the Warfighter tremendously. He participated in numerous highly successful Corps, Brigade, Division and Joint exercises.

From 1995 - 1996, Mr. Cornwall was selected to be the G6 Network Management Technician, 2nd Infantry Division (M), Camp Red Cloud, Korea. With his vast technical knowledge, he introduced packet switch and data networking to the division. He also upgraded all MSE switches to ESOP in 2nd ID. From 1996 - 2000, he was the Senior Network Management Technician, HHC 3rd Signal Brigade, Fort Hood, TX. He provided technical assistance and oversight of the proof of concept of the highly successful first digitized Brigade, Division and Corps fielding's and deployment. Due to his network knowledge as an architect, designer, planner and troubleshooter the Division Advance Warfighting Experiment was a tremendous success.

From 2000 - 2001, he was the Senior Network Management Technician, III Corps G6, Fort Hood, TX. His expertise allowed for a successful Corps Warfighter and numerous other very highly successful Exercises and NTC rotations. From 2001 - 2002, he was selected to participate in the Training with Industry (TWI) program with General Dynamics, Taunton, MA. He was a major player in the development of the Vantage Switch, the concept of Voice over Internet Protocol and its deployment into the tactical force. He was one of the founding integrators for the initial concept of WIN-T Inc 1 & 2 Joint Network Node, CPN and on the move network (OTM).

From 2002 – 2005, he was assigned as the Chief Network Engineer of the Directorate of Combat Development (DCD) at the US Army Signal Center. His influence while working the BBN, MSE/TRITAC Program Improvement Plan, and Task Force – Network, Joint Network Node (JNN), WIN-T Increments and numerous other projects allowed the Signal Corp to provide better Signal support to meet the War Fighters requirements. From 2005- 2008, he served as the Chief Integrator and Senior Technical Advisor to the Director TRADOC Integration Office and Capabilities Development and Integration Directorate US Army Signal Center.

From 2008 to 2012, CW5 Cornwall served as the Command Senior Chief Warrant Officer for the 7th Signal Command (Theater). As such, he was the senior warrant advisor to the Commander of the 7th Signal Command (Theater) on any and all issues that affected all Signal warrants from the three Brigades under the Command. During his tenure as the Command Senior Chief Warrant he influenced the standardization and configuration management across the Operating and Generating Force in the CONUS Theater. CW5 Cornwall was hand-picked to deploy to Afghanistan as the Senior Network Integrator responsible for optimizing the transport network for the Combined Joint Operations Area- Afghanistan. His influence and expertise allowed for Combatant Commanders to see the full spectrum of operations via the Afghan Mission Network.

CW5 Cornwall traveled extensively to coach and mentor Warrant Officers from all branches. He always put the needs of junior Warrant Officers above his own making sure they were always taken care of with respect. He was always available to all Warrants even those he knew nothing about to discuss the unique issues of the WO Corps. He never missed an occasion to discuss the opportunities of being of WO with enlisted personnel.

CW5 Cornwall's wealth of knowledge and leadership was sought after by many of his subordinates and peers. Whenever a new project was on the horizon for the Signal Corps Rank Name was always asked to participate. He was a vital role in the decision making process for any Signal Corps initiatives that enabled the Warfighter to communicate more effectively.

CW5 Cornwall's awards and commendations include the Legion of Merit, Meritorious Service Medal (6 awards), Army Commendation Medal (6 awards), Army Achievement Medal (8 awards), and numerous other Military awards.

He was selected as a Distinguished Member of the Signal Regiment and received the Bronze and Silver Orders of Mercury.

Even in retirement CW5 Cornwall continues to support this great Army and Signal Regiment as a Senior Strategy and Business development Manager for General Dynamics Mission Systems supporting numerous DoD programs.

CW5 Cornwall has brought distinct credit upon himself, the Signal Regiment, and the United States Army.

Chief Warrant Officer Five James E. Davis

Chief Warrant Officer Five James E. Davis is the USARC Engineer Tech for Army Reserve Installations around the country and different parts of the world while stationed here at Fort Bragg, North Carolina.

CW5 Davis holds an Executive Masters in Business Administration from Howard University in Washington DC, a Bachelors in Business Administration from Prairie View A&M University in Prairie View Texas and a Project Management Professional - PMP Certificate from George Washington University.

His civilian experience includes sixteen years at Hewlett Packard as a Project Manager in addition to his current endeavors as a Franchisee in the restaurant industry. He also served as the Mid-Southern Region Director of the U.S. Army Warrant Officer Association.

CW5 Davis' professional military education includes 14 weeks of Logistics training at Fort Lee Virginia, Engineer Warrant Officer Basic and Advance Courses at Fort Leonard Wood and Fort Belvoir respectively, in addition to U.S. Army Warrant Officer Senior Staff Education at Fort Rucker Alabama. While enlisted he served on active duty from '80-83 and deployed to Desert Storm in '91 with the 808th Pipeline Engineer Company.

His assignments include Platoon Leader, Maintenance Officer and Field Hospital Maintenance Officer at the 94th General Hospital in Seagoville Texas; Platoon Leader, Maintenance Officer and Field Hospital Maintenance Officer at the 228th Combat Support Hospital at Fort Sam Houston Texas before deployment to Iraq; Logistics Technician at the 75th G4 at Old Spanish Trail now located at

Ellington Field in southwest Houston; Contracting Officer responsibilities of several multimillion dollar labor and construction contracts at 1st Army Division West Fort Hood Texas in support of deploying detachments, companies, battalions and brigades; Special Mission OIC for Warrant Officer recruitment in 12th Battalion Army Reserve Careers Division in Grand Prairie Texas; Construction Engineer Technician at OCAR in the Facility Policy and Operations Divisions respectively at Fort Belvoir Virginia; Operations Officer in Human Capital OCAR G1, Fort Belvoir Virginia; Regional Engineer Technician at the 99th Reserve Support Command Department of Public Works and Deputy Military Director of the 99th DPW, Joint Base McGuire Dix Lakehurst, New Jersey; USARC Engineer Technician, Fort Bragg, North Carolina.

CW5 Davis' major awards and decorations include the Meritorious Service Medal (3OLC), ARCM (2OLC), AAM (2OLC), AR-Comp-ACHVMT-MDL-5, NATL-DEF-SVC-MDL (2 BSDev), SW-ASIA-SM-BSS(2), GWOTSM, GWOTEM, AFRM-M 3 (30yr Res), NCO Prof Dev RBN-3, Army SVC RBN, OS-SVC-RBN(2), ARCOTR, CW5 Davis' honorary awards include the Army Staff Identification Badge.

CW5 Davis' wife Gennifer, and daughter Gillian (11) reside in Houston, his son Titus (13) attends Hargrave Military Academy in Chatham Virginia. Daughter, Gabrielle currently serving on active duty in the Air Force and son is serving in the Army Reserve. James Spencer and Latoya both reside in Texas as well.

Chief Warrant Officer Five Artavia M. Edwards

Chief Warrant Officer Five Artavia M. Edwards serves as the Chief Legal Administrator, California Army National Guard, providing senior staff level MOS Proponency and decision-making functions, contemporaneously responsible for national actions concerning manpower, authorizations, and 270A MOS Legal Administrators for recruitment, while collaborating with coordinating the goals of NGB-JA Chief Counsel, with NGB CCWO, and State CCWOs, with dual responsibility for assisting the State Staff Judge Advocate in the total delivery of legal services in the California Army National Guard.

CW5 Edwards has a Juris Doctor degree, a Master of Science degree in Leadership, a Bachelor of Science degree in Business Administration, an Associate of Arts Degree in General Business, and is currently a doctoral student; is a graduate from Airborne and Master Fitness Trainer Schools; served as a Notary Public from 1988 to present; served as a Notary Ambassador, Sacramento, National Notary Association from 1994-2006; is a trained Parliamentarian and member of the National Association of Parliamentarians; is a registered Mediator; is Captain of the California National Guard Marathon Team; competed as a member of Team USA in the July 2011 World Masters Athletics Championships; and is a Martial Artist, Red/Black Belt, and will receive a Black Belt in Taekwondo in 2018, and received gold medals for her performance in State and National Taekwondo Championships from 2015-2017.

CW5 Edwards' military awards and decorations include the Legion of Merit, Meritorious Service Medal (with Oak Leaf Cluster); the Army Commendation Medal (with Oak Leaf Cluster); the Army Achievement Medal; the Army Reserve Components Achievement

Meal (with 2 Oak Leaf Clusters); the National Defense Service Medal (with 1 Bronze Star); the Armed Forces Reserve Medal; the Non-Commissioned Officer Professional Development Ribbon; the Army Service Ribbon; and the USAR Unit Pewter Cup Award.

Chief Warrant Officer Five Janice L. Fontanez

Chief Warrant Officer Five Janice L. Fontanez assumed her duties as the Senior Signal Warrant Officer, Advisor Army National Guard (ARNG) CIO/G6, National Guard Bureau (NGB) July 2013. As the Senior Signal Warrant Officer ARNG CIO/G6 she provides leadership, guidance, mentorship, technical input and direction on information systems, networks, cyber operations, governance and polices to senior leaders, Warrant Officers, and non-commissioned officers in the ARNG.

CW5 Fontanez began her military career began August, 1975, when she enlisted in the United States Army Reserve, in Athens, Georgia. She later joined the District of Columbia ARNG in July, 1978. CW5 Fontanez served in the enlisted ranks, rising to rank of Sergeant First Class as a member of Headquarters, District Area Command. In 1989, she attended Warrant Officer Candidate School at Fort McCoy, Wisconsin. CW5 Fontanez received her appointment as WO1 November, 1989 at Fort Gordon, Georgia after completing Signal Warrant Officer Basic Course. CW5 Fontanez served in varies assignments from 1989 – 2003 while serving in the District of Columbia ARNG. Her duty assignments included System Programmer/Analyst, Telecommunication Manager, and Information Management Branch Chief.

In 2003, CW5 Fontanez was accepted in the Active Guard Reserve (AGR) Title 10 program, supporting the ARNG CIO/G6 directorate as the Guard Knowledge Online (GKO) Webmaster, where she managed resources, personnel, architecture and design of GKO secure and non-secure portals capabilities. In 2009, she served as the ARNG Enterprise Chief Computer Network Defense (CND) and was responsible for coordination and execution of the ARNG Information Assurance and CND program for GuardNet XXI. In 2011, CW5 Fontanez was selected as the Senior Signal Warrant Officer Advisor ARNG, TRADOC Command, Signal Center of Excellence, Fort Gordon, Georgia. As the Senior Signal Warrant Officer advisor ARNG, she was the principle advisor to the Deputy Assistant Commandant ARNG, 442nd Signal BN Cyber Leader College on all Reserve Component actions; advisor to NGB Command Chief Warrant Officer (CCWO), 54 states, territories and the District of Columbia CCWO's on Signal training and education. Her civilian education includes a Bachelor of Arts degree in Business Management.

CW5 Fontanez's military decorations include the Meritorious Service Medal (with 3 Bronze Oak Leaf Clusters), Army Commendation Medal (With 1 Bronze Oak Leaf Cluster), Army Achievement Medal, Army Service Ribbon, Armed Forces Reserve Medal (With Gold Hourglass), National Defense Medal (With Bronze Service Star), Non-Commissioned Officer Professional Development Ribbon (With Numeral 3), Global War on Terrorism Expeditionary Medal, and the United States Army Signal Regiment Bronze Order of Mercury.

Master Warrant Officer Four David H. Ford, Sr., Retired

David H. Ford, Sr. Master Warrant Officer Four (MW4) was born in Cartersville, Georgia in March 1944. He attended school in Cartersville and graduated from Main High School, Rome, Georgia in 1961. David graduated from Floyd College and later attended Troy State University and the University of Maryland, European Division majoring in Business Administration.

Ford enlisted in the United States Army on 16 July 1962 and completed basic and advanced military training at the US Army Armor Training Center and School, Fort Knox, Kentucky. After attaining the rank of Sergeant and completing an assignment in the Republic of Vietnam, David received a direct appointment as a Quartermaster Warrant Officer in 1968. Ford graduated from the Supply Management Officers Course, US Army Logistics Management Agency, Standard Army Retail Supply System Course, Division Automated Supply and Support Course, US Army Quartermaster Center and School, Fort Lee, Virginia, Chief Warrant Officer Senior Course and the Master Warrant Officer Training Course held at the US Army Aviation Center and School, Fort Rucker, Alabama.

Ford was one of the first three African American Chief Warrant Officers selected by Department of The Army for attendance at the Master Warrant Officer Career College. Ford's awards and decorations include the Legion of Merit, Bronze Star Medal, Meritorious Service Medal w/3 OLCs, Army Commendation Medal W/2 OLCs, Army Achievement Medal w/OLC, Good Conduct Medal w/OLC, National Defense Service Medal, Vietnam Service Medal with five service stars, Army Service Ribbon, Overseas Service Ribbon, and the Republic of Vietnam Campaign Medal.

During Ford's military career, he served during the Vietnam War, Operation Desert Shield/Storm and numerous overseas assignments in Europe and Asia. David held a wide variety of high level logistics and staff positions throughout the United States and overseas culminating his military career and retirement in June 1994 as a System Integrator/Logistics Staff Officer, Assistant Chief of Staff, G4, XVIII Airborne Corps, Fort Bragg, North Carolina.

Ford is a life member of the Military Officers Association, Association of the US Army, a Life member of the Disabled Veterans Association, U.S. Army Quartermaster Association, and a member of American Legion Post 506.

David is married to the former Barbara Gibbons and they have five children, Amanda, David Jr., Terry, Jeffery, and Joey. The Ford's have twelve grandchildren and 6 great-grandchildren.

Chief Warrant Officer Five Michael D. Gamble

CW5 Gamble entered the US Army in 1985 from hometown of Montgomery Alabama. While enlisted, he served as a mechanic, platoon sergeant and motor sergeant. His assignments included the 38th Signal & 237th Engineers West Germany, 1-10th Calvary & 530th Maintenance Fort Knox, and 1-10th Aviation Fort Rucker.

Mr. Gamble was appointed a WO1 in 1994. He served in leadership / functional positions including Unit / Battalion / Brigade /Support Maintenance Officer, Logistics Officer/Advisor, Liaison Team Chief, Contracting Officer's Representative and Inspector General. His assignments included the 1-501st Aviation & 2nd Forward Support, South Korea; 36th Engineers Fort Benning; 426th Forward Support 101st Assault Division, Fort Campbell; 120thTraining Support & 201st Brigade Support, Fort Hood, 3rd US Infantry (The Old Guard), Fort Myer; Army Inspector General Agency & Corps of Engineers, Washington, DC. His combat tours include Iraqi and Afghanistan.

CW5 Gamble's military education includes the Warrant Officer Entry through the Warrant Officer Senior Staff Courses, Joint/Multinational Logistics Courses, Force Integration Course, Instructor Training Course, Airborne/Air Assault Courses and Master Fitness Trainer Course.

He earned a Bachelor's Degree in Resources Management from Troy University and MBA in Public Management from Touro University with honors. CW5 Gamble is a designed Demonstrated Master Logistician by the International Society of Logistics.

Mr. Gamble's awards/decorations include Bronze Star Medals, Meritorious Service Medals, Army Commendation Medals, Ordnance Order of Samuel Sharpe Award and more.

Chief Warrant Officer Five Gamble is a Past Chapter President/Lifetime member of the USAWOA Fort Hood Silver Chapter and an American Legion member.

Chief Warrant Officer Three (Retired) James P. Gillespie, 270A, Legal Administrator

Born and raised in Louisville, Kentucky, I graduated from Louisville Male High School in 1983. I enlisted in the US Navy in 1985. I completed boot camp in Orlando, Florida then graduated from Machinist Mate "A" in 1986. After MM "A" School, my primary job in the Navy was designated in the ship's engineering and main propulsion systems. My first assignment was the aircraft carrier USS Midway CV-41 stationed in Yokosuka, Japan. In 1988, I transferred to Guam aboard the Submarine Tender USS Proteus AS-19.

In 1991, I attended the Law Enforcement Academy at Lackland Air Force Base. After graduation, I achieved a secondary job in Navy. My next assignment was at Cubic Point Naval Air Station in the Republic of the Philippines. Cubic Point closed in 1992; I transferred to Pearl Harbor Naval Station, Hawaii. I honorably discharged from the Navy in 1996. My spouse and I returned to Louisville, Kentucky.

In 2000, I enlisted in the Army Reserves with a designation of unqualified military paralegal. I was assigned to 139th Legal Support Organization (LSO) located in Louisville, Kentucky under the 81st Regional Readiness Command. In 2003, the 139th LSO was mobilized in support of Global War on Terrorism. I was stationed at Camp Atterbury's Office of the Staff Judge Advocate, Edinburgh, Indiana. I went to 27D Paralegal School at Fort Jackson, South Carolina in 2003; thereby becoming a qualified military paralegal.

I returned to Camp Atterbury and remained mobilized until accepting an Active-Guard Reserve position with the 213th LSO. During my period of mobilization, I participated and graduated from

Primary Leadership Development Course, Basic Noncommissioned Officer Course Phase I, Pre-Warrant Officer Candidate School, Warrant Officer Candidate School, Warrant Officer Basic Course, 2008 Warrant Officer Judge Advocate Triennial Training Course, 2010 Warrant Officer Advance Course, Reassigned to 8th LOD October 2011; final assignment 154th LOD-TDS October 2014.

Transitioned via Fort Belvoir, VA October 2017; Fort Belvoir, Virginia Retirement Ceremony; Final DD Form214 31DEC2017; MSA-HRA Human Resources Graduation from Central Michigan University 16DEC2017.

Retired 20180101.

Chief Warrant Officer Three (Retired) Jacqueline E. Gaddis

CW3 (Ret) Jacqueline E Gaddis is an Alabama native and began her military career in September of 1977 when she enlisted into the Regular Army, as a truck driver. She received her commission as a Warrant Officer from Warrant Officer Candidate School at Fort Rucker, Alabama in February 1997. She was the second black female warrant officer to be appointed in the state of AL was well as the fourth female warrant officer in the state. She holds an Associate in Applied Science degree from Vincennes University.

CW3 (Ret) Gaddis retired March 31, 2004 from the Alabama Army National Guard with a total of 26 years' service. Her assignments included Military Personnel Technician/Branch Chief, HQS Starc AL ARNG, Montgomery, AL from 1997 through 2004. While serving as Branch Chief she also held additional duties as TAC Officer for the Alabama Warrant Officer Pre Candidate Course at Ft McClellan, Alabama. She was the first black female as well as the only black female TAC officer to serve in this position. She later became the first and only black Senior TAC Officer as well as the Commandant for the Warrant Officer Pre Candidate Couse while serving in this position until she retired.

CW3 (Ret) Gaddis military awards and decorations include the Meritorious Service Medal, Army Commendation Medal, Army Achievement Medal with two Bronze Oak Leaf Clusters, Good Conduct Medal with 3 Bronze knots, Army Reserve Component Achievement Medal with two Bronze Oak Leaf Clusters, National Defense Service Medal with one Bronze Star, Global War on Terrorism Service Ribbon, Humanitarian Service Medal, Armed Forces Reserve Medal with Silver Hour Glass, Non-Commissioned

Officer Professional Development Ribbon with 3 Numeral, Army Service Ribbon, Overseas Service Ribbon, Army Reserve Components Overseas Training Ribbon with 3 Numeral, Veterans Service Medal of Alabama, Special Service Medal of Alabama, Faithful Service Medal of Alabama with Four Bronze Saint Andrews Crosses, and Drivers Badge.

CW3 (Ret) Gaddis reside in Montgomery, Alabama and has a son (Mario Gaddis).

CW2 Gaddis with a WOC candidate

Chief Warrant Officer Four Destria Denise Gladney
OCRA Liaison

CW4 Destria Gladney is currently assigned as the Liaison, for the Reserve Proponency Chief of Transportation, headquartered Fort Lee Petersburg, Virginia. Her Active Guard Reserve (AGR) assignments include twelve years of active duty. She served as Division Transportation Officer, 412th Theater Engineer Command, Vicksburg, Mississippi "13-17", Senior Mobility Warrant Officer, 310th Expeditionary Sustainment Command (ESC) Indianapolis, Indiana "06-13", as well as, Assistant Deployment Support Chief for Military Surface Deployment and Distribution Command in Fort Eustis, Virginia "04-06" prior to their transition to Scott Air Force Base, Illinois. Prior to transitioning to active duty in the U.S. Army Guard Reserve in 2006, Chief Destria Gladney held positions of leadership in the 1397th Deployment & Distribution Support Battalion, as Cargo Documentation Team Lead and 483d Transportation Battalion, Mobilization Chief. Her assignments have included the 63RD Regional Support Command (RSC), 511th Movement Control Team, and 377th Theater Sustainment Command, 310th Sustainment Command (Expeditionary) (ESC).

CW4 Gladney is a graduate of the Warrant Officer Staff Course, Warrant Officer Senior Enhancement Staff Course and Senior Transportation Officer Qualification 90A Course. She holds a Bachelor of Arts in Sociology from California State University, Sacramento, California, Associates of Art, in Psychology with a focus on Drug Behavior, and certifications in various fields as Paralegal Studies, Social Services, Transportation management, Knowledge, and

Project Management, to include obtaining an Additional Skill Identifier (ASI) of 8R, Master Resiliency Trainer (MRT).

CW4 Gladney's deployments include Southwest Asia, with the 511th Movement Control Team, Kuwait with the Military Surface Distribution and Deployment Command, and Iraq in the position of Theater Container Manager in which the 310th ESC closed down Joint Base Balad in 2011.

Her awards and decorations include the Meritorious Service Medal (with 2 Oak Leaf Clusters), the Army Commendation Medal (with Silver and Bronze Oak Leaf Clusters), the Army Achievement Medal, National Defense Service Medal, Global War on Terrorism Expeditionary Medal, and Global War on Terrorism Service Medal, Overseas Service Medal, and Meritorious Unit Commendation.

CW4 Gladney is community oriented, and has served as an Executive Officer American Legion, Tyner Ford #213, Vicksburg, MS, Ordained Exhorter, and Elder at Transforming Life Church, Indianapolis, Indiana, and Youth Leader at Word of Faith Christian Church, Vicksburg, Mississippi, and a Certified Layman with Bruised Reed Ministries. Chief Gladney holds recognition in the United States Army Reserves as the First Senior Mobility Warrant, as well as, Cambridge Who's Who; Elite Women in America, and Top Female Executives, Professionals & Entrepreneurs.

Chief Warrant Officer Three (Retired) Julius Green

Mr. Julius Green has an impressive past and present. One of the most significant is his service to our nation during some challenging times historically. Mr. Green was the United States Army's first African American Diver. A job that required remarkable physical and mental strength beyond the limits of what most deems to be extraordinary. His ability to ensure these difficulties culminated in him obtaining the prestige of Master Diver. It also was the catapult to other successes forthcoming.

Julius Green started his journey having completed only a tenth-grade education. He joined the United States Army in 1951. After he completed Basic Combat Training he was stationed in Germany for three years. Following his tour in Germany, he was stationed in Fort Jackson, South Carolina where he applied and was accepted to train to become a U.S. Army Diver. The irony is at the time he did not know how to swim.

In 1956 upon completing the training at the U.S Amy's Diving school in Fort Eustis, Virginia, Julius Green became only the second African American diver in the U.S. military and the first in the U.S. Army having obtained the Noncommissioned Officer's (NCO) rank of Sergeant First Class (E-7), Sergeant Green applied and was accepted to the US Army Marine Engineering Warrant Officer's Basic Course. Upon graduation Mr. Julius Green became the Army's first African-American Diving Officer.

Mr. Green served as an instructor in the Army Diving Training Program at Fort Eustis until his retirement as a Chief Warrant Officer 3 in 1973. His Army service also included two combat tours in Vietnam from 1967-68 and 1970-1971. After 22 years of service in the

U.S. military, Mr. Green retired from the U.S. Army on October 31, 1973.

He has earned an Associate's Degree and a Bachelor's Degree from Saint Leo University. His post Army retirement took him to the College of William & Mary in Williamsburg, Virginia where he was employed for 23 years. He retired from that career as the Director of Operations for the College in 1996.

Julius Green has been an extremely active person in his community. He is a life member of the Sigma Delta Chapter of Phi Beta Sigma Fraternity, Inc. He has been a Freemason since 1956, is a Past Master of Pioneer Lodge No 315, Free & Accepted Masons, Prince Hall Affiliation and has held other local, state, and national offices. He has also served as President of the U.S. Army Diver's Association. He is a Deacon at his church in Newport News Virginia where he lives with his wife Rosalyn and they share two children, two grandchildren and their great grandchildren.

Mr. Julius Green lives a victorious and courageous life. His contributions will last for years to come and show all no matter the circumstances; one can achieve great successes even during hardships.

In April 2018 the 100 Black Men, Virginia Peninsula Chapter, honored Mr. Green with the group's Trailblazer Award.

Chief Warrant Officer Five Cory K. Hill

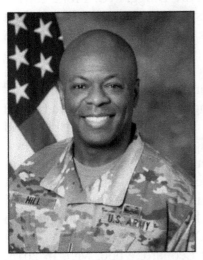

CW5 Corey K. Hill, a native of Scotland Neck, North Carolina, began his career as a Private in July 1987. Upon completion of Basic Combat Training and Advanced Individual Training as a Plumbing Specialist at Fort Leonard Wood, Missouri, he was assigned to the 558th Transportation Company as a Pipefitter at Fort Eustis, Virginia. From 1988 – 1993, he had assignments serving as a Plumber / Pipefitter with Charlie Company, 802nd Engineer Battalion (CH) at Camp Humphreys, Korea, HHC, 588th Engineer Battalion (C) and Charlie Company, 34th Engineer Battalion (CH) at Fort Polk, Louisiana. In 1990, he deployed to Iraq in support of Operations Desert Storm / Shield. From 1993 – 2000, CW5 Hill served as Assistant Squad Leader, Squad Leader, Platoon Sergeant, Company Operations Sergeant, First Sergeant, Battalion Training NCO and Battalion Vertical Construction NCOIC. During this period, he was assigned to Bravo Company, 84th Engineer Battalion (CH) in Schofield Barracks, Hawaii where he deployed to Thailand, Haiti, and Laos in support of Operations Cobra Gold, Uphold Democracy, and Joint Task Force Full Accounting respectively. His next assignment took him to Fort Stewart, Georgia as part of Alpha Company, 92nd Engineer Battalion (CH). While at Fort Stewart, he deployed to Egypt in support of Operation Bright Star 1999 and advanced to the rank of Sergeant First Class. In March 2000, he made his final move as an enlisted soldier to Fort Wainwright, Alaska where he served with HQ, United States Army Adjutant General's Office as Installation Management NCOIC.

In September 2000, CW5 Hill was selected for Warrant Officer Candidate School. He graduated and was appointed as a Warrant Officer One on 19 December 2000. After completion of Warrant

Officer Basic Course, he was assigned to Bravo Company, 249th Engineer Battalion (Prime Power) at Fort Bragg, NC. From 2001 – 2009, CW5 Hill served as a Power Systems Technician / Detachment Commander with the 249th in various positions at multiple CONUS and OCONUS locations. While at Fort Bragg, he deployed to Afghanistan in support of Operations Enduring Freedom and Iraqi Freedom in 2001 and 2003. Upon returning in 2004, he moved to 4th Detachment, Alpha Company, 249th Engineer Battalion (Prime Power) in Camp Humphreys, Korea. In 2006, he returned to Fort Bragg and Bravo Company, 249th Engineer Battalion (Prime Power).

In 2008, he deployed his detachment in support of Operation Iraqi Freedom. In 2009, CW5 Hill was reassigned to the 28th Combat Support Hospital where he deployed in support of Operations Iraqi Freedom/New Dawn. As of July 2011, he was assigned to the position of Deputy Chief, Engineer Personnel Development Office (EPDO) at the US Army Engineer School on Fort Leonard Wood, MO. In 2013, CW5 Hill was selected to serve as the Directorate of EPDO and subsequently appointed in 2015 as Interim Engineer Regimental Chief Warrant Officer of the US Army Engineer School and Regiment. In September 2015, he became the Commander / Deputy Commandant of the US Army Prime Power School, US Army Corps of Engineers, where he currently serves.

CW5 Hill's Enlisted Professional Military Education includes Primary Leadership Development Course (1990), Basic Non Commissioned Officer's Course (1993) and Advanced Non Commissioned Officer's Course (2000). His Warrant Officer Professional Military Education includes Warrant Officer Candidate School (2000), Warrant Officer Basic Course (2001), Warrant Officer Advanced Course (2006), Warrant Officer Staff Course (2011) and Warrant Officer Senior Staff Course (2014). He also completed the Master Fitness Trainer Course and Air Assault Qualification Course.

CW5 Hill's civilian education includes attending Central Texas College where he received an Associates of Science (AS) degree in Business Management. He subsequently attended Park University receiving a Bachelor of Science (BS) degree in Management / Engineering Administration. He received a Master of Art (MA) degree in Management and Leadership from Webster University in December 2016.

Over 30 years of military service, CW5 Hill has achieved a number of awards and decoration, those of which include the Bronze Star Medal (1OLC), Meritorious Service Medal (4OLC), Army Commendation Medal (6OLC), Army Achievement Medal (5OLC), Army Good Conduct Medal (4), National Defense Service Medal, Armed Forces Expeditionary Medal (1), Southwest Asia Service Medal (3BS), Iraq Campaign Medal-Campaign Stars (3), Global War on Terrorism Expeditionary Medal, Global War on Terrorism Service Medal, Korea Defense Service Medal, Humanitarian Service Medal, Non Commissioned Officer Professional Development Ribbon (Numeral 3), Army Service Ribbon, Overseas Ribbon, Southwest Asia Kuwait Liberation Medal, Air Assault Badge and Drivers / Mechanics Badge.

CW5 Hill was promoted to the prestigious rank of Chief Warrant Officer Five on 9 November 2016. He shares this coveted honor with his beautiful wife Chanel and their children, Cortney, Christen, Cameryn, and Jordyn.

Fundamental Philosophy: Collaborative Efforts Strengthen the Ability and Power to Succeed

Values and principles begin and end with a grounded faith in God. They are stabilized by the love and support of family. They are guided by the honor of being a selfless servant. They are driven by the ability to pay it forward to the next generation of leaders as a legacy of longevity that contributes to team success.

Chief Warrant Officer Four (Retired) Jelpher Hillsman

Jelpher Hillsman, born in 1963 to the late James and Bobbie Hillsman in Nashville, Tennessee, served with distinction in the U.S. Army for over 28 years (1983-2011). He began in the enlisted ranks in 1983, making Staff Sergeant, then progressed into aviation, becoming a Unit Senior Instructor, Unit Instrument Examiner, Platoon Leader and Flight Commander before retiring as a CW4. In that time, for his proficiency as a UH-60 and OH-58 Scout Pilot he was awarded with the Army Commendation Medal, the Air Medal, and the Master Aviator Badge. In addition to his numerous medals, he earned the Southwest Asia Service Medal with two Bronze Stars for his distinguished participation in the Gulf War. His education and experience encompassed not just the demanded requirements of aviation, but also the Warrant Officer Aviation Advance Course, the Aero-scout Instructor Pilot's Course, the Senior Warrant Officer Advance Course, and the Rotary Wing Instrument Examiner Course.

As Flight Commander for U.S. American and Foreign Military Basic Combat Skills Training, his duties facilitated the management, implementation and reporting of the commander's Aircrew Training Program, as well as maintaining the standards and evaluating the proficiency of over 40 staff aviators. At the time of his service as one of the few black Flight Commanders serving in Fort Rucker and later as the only black Flight Commander for a civilian contractor at Fort Rucker, he capably conducted the standardized training of rated/non-rated aviators in Day/Night/NVG phases of Basic Combat skills while also teaching maneuvers such as terrain flight operations, low-level, contour, nap-of-the-earth, non-standard maneuvers and emergency maneuvers.

Dr. Harry L. Hobbs - Chief Warrant Officer Five (Retired)
Florida Institute of Technology Huntsville/Redstone Site Director

Dr. Harry Hobbs was selected to be the Site Director for the Florida Institute of Technology Huntsville/Redstone site on February 17, 2017

Career Assignments

U.S. Army Soldier / Chief Warrant Officer Five: 1978 - 2007

Adjunct Professor at Florida Institute of Technology: 2007 - Present

Professor of Military Science JROTC Columbia High School: 2007 - 2010

Police Communications Relations Officer: 2010 – 2014

Community Relations Liaison/Education Officer Huntsville Utilities: 2014 - 2017

Civilian Education:

Florida Institute of Technology Doctorate in Business Administration

Doctorate Degree in Human Resources Management from Pacific Western University, Honolulu, Hawaii

Master of Science degree in Human Services, Murray State University, Kentucky

Bachelor of Science degree in Resources Management, Troy State at Dothan, Alabama

Associate of Science degree in Missile and Munitions Technology, John C. Calhoun State College, Decatur, Alabama

Dr. Hobbs retired from the U.S. Army in 2007 with over 29 years of military service. He then became the Professor of Military Science of the (JROTC) program at Columbia High School in Huntsville,

Alabama from 2007-2010. In 2010 Dr. Hobbs was selected to be the Communications Relations Officer for the Huntsville, Alabama Police Department until 2014. He was selected as the youth mentor of the year by the 100 Black Men Organization in 2011. He was selected as the city of Madison Veteran of the year 2012. In 2013 he was inducted into the U.S. Army Ordnance Corps Hall of Fame, the first Missile Systems Warrant Officer in the history of the Army. In January 2104 he was presented the 2014 Martin Luther King Unity Award, in February 2014 he was presented the Whitney M. Young Community Service Award from the Boy Scouts of America and in May 2016 he was presented the city of Huntsville's "Racial Harmony" award.

Chief Warrant Officer Three Linda R. Horton

Chief Warrant Officer Three Linda R. Horton, a native of Washington, North Carolina, is the daughter of Glenwood and Sue Horton. She joined the 213th Military Police Company in the North Carolina National Guard (NCNG), in 1989, after leaving Fayetteville State University (FSU) in Fayetteville, NC. In 1988 she married and had two lovely children Calvin and Brittany Woolard.

In 2003, she was selected to support the State Partnership Peace Training in Moldova, Eastern Europe. She deployed in support of Operation Iraqi Freedom 2003-2005. In 2013, she was selected to command the 440th Army Band, the first African American female to hold this position. She arrived at the unit during a time of turmoil and immediately began to bring stability to the organization. Her efforts culminated in receiving the Meritorious Service Medal Award at the end of her tour.

Ms. Horton was the first to receive, from the state of North Carolina, the coveted National Guard Eagle Rising Award for her outstanding leadership and contributions to the Warrant Officer Community from the National Guard Association of the United States (NGAUS), 2016. As a NCNG Executive Council Member from 2015 to 2017, her contributions to the residents of North Carolina earned her the President's Award in 2016.

She is currently working as a uniformed Human Resources Supervisor in the HRO office for the NCNG with over 18 years over service.

Her dedication and contributions extend beyond the military sector. In her civilian life, she tutors and mentors local students and enjoys participating in read-ins and career day programs for students at the local school.

She is the first female to hold the position of Commander of the American Legion Post 518, Clayton, North Carolina.

Her philosophy in life is, "as veterans we are blessed to have the opportunity to give to others, our time and resources. My joy is giving and not expecting anything in return". She is a member of Alpha Kappa Alpha Sorority, Inc. She now serves as the secretary for Raleigh-Wake Federal State University Alumni Chapter and is a member of Kingdom Life Church in Washington, North Carolina.

Chief Horton currently resides in Garner, North Carolina and enjoys spending time with her grandsons, Blake and Carson.

Chief Warrant Officer Five Billy Jackson

Chief Warrant Officer Five Billy Jackson is currently assigned to the Army Test and Evaluation Command, Army Evaluation Center, Aberdeen Proving Ground, Maryland as the Senior Military Technical Evaluator.

He enlisted in to the Army in 1983 at Fort Sill, Oklahoma. In 1992 he was appointed to the rank of Warrant Officer One after completing the Warrant Officer's Air Defense Maintenance Technical Training at Fort Bliss, Texas in 1992.

Mr. Jackson served as the Warrant Officer Senior Advisor to the Commanding Generals of the Army Sustainment Command and the 21st Theater Sustainment Command, Kaiserslautern, Germany. He holds a Master of Science degree in Information Technology Management from Trident University International, Cypress, California and a BS in Business Management from Fayetteville State University, Fayetteville, North Carolina. He is a graduate of the Warrant Officer Basic and Advanced Courses, the Warrant Officer Staff Course, and the Warrant Officer Senior Staff Course. Mr. attended the Army Sustainment Command Senior Leaders Workshop at the University of North Carolina at Chapel Hill, Kenan-Flagler Business School and is a Demonstrated Master Logistician.

CW5 Jackson served in Operation Iraq Freedom and Operation Enduring Freedom in Southwest Asia. His awards and decorations include the Legion of Merit, Bronze Star Medal, Meritorious Service Medal with 4 Oak Leaf Clusters, Army Commendation Medal with 3 Oak Leaf Clusters, and Army Achievement Medal with 3 Oak Leaf Clusters.

Photo: CW5 Owens (left) presents a gift to
CW5 Jackson for being his mentor.

Chief Warrant Officer Four James H. Johnson

Chief Warrant Officer Four James Johnson is a native of Florida. He entered the Army as a trumpet player in 1979, but soon after his musical notes would soar above the rest as his military career was destined for the high skies.

During his first assignment with the 434th U.S. Army Signal Corps Band at Fort Gordon, Georgia, he exceled to the rank of Staff Sergeant before being assigned as a trumpet section leader with the 2nd Infantry Division Band at Camp Casey, Korea. It was there he discovered his interest in aviation.

In 1985, he submitted his application to become an Army Warrant Officer Aviator. He was selected and assigned to attend the Warrant Officer Candidate School at Fort Rucker, Alabama with flight training to follow. While attending flight school, he was assigned the "Scout Track" OH58A/C airframe. On 6 December 1986 he was appointed a Warrant Officer and the following day he was awarded his Army Aviator Badge (Pilot Wings.) In 1988, Chief Warrant Officer Four Johnson went on to complete the Aviation Safety Officers Course.

Throughout his more than 38-year military career, Chief Warrant Officer Four Johnson has served in a wide variety of leadership positions in a multitude of active and reserve Army commands. He deployed overseas twice in support of Operations Desert Shield, Storm and Provide Comfort. He has served as a scout helicopter pilot, utility helicopter pilot, aviation safety manager, night vision device maintainer, army warrant officer recruiter and assistant operations (S-3) and (S-4) logistics officer.

Chief Warrant Officer Four Johnson holds a commercial pilot license, both airplane and helicopter. He has amassed more than 8,000 flight hours throughout his military and civilian career.

In August 2007, he was awarded the ALEA (Airborne Law Enforcement Association) Aircrew of the Year Award and in 2012 he retired from the Metro Nashville Police Department, where he was the Chief Pilot in Nashville, Tennessee.

Chief Warrant Officer Four Johnson has a Master's Degree in Management and is a graduate of the Warrant Officer Staff Course.

His military awards and decorations include the Senior Army Aviator Badge, Meritorious Service Medal, the Army Air Medal, Army Commendation Medals, Army Achievement Medals, Army Good Conduct Medals, the National Defense Service Medal, the Southwest Asia Campaign Medal and the Kuwait Liberation Medal.

He is married and has two daughters, Ashley Johnson and Amber Smith.

Chief Warrant Officer Four Adrian L. Levett

A native of Tuskegee, Alabama, in May 1990 to September 1990, Mr. Levett attended basic training at Fort Leonard Wood and AIT at Fort Jackson as an Administrative Specialist. On October 1990, he was assigned to the 167th DPU of the Alabama Army National Guard (AL-ARNG). June 1992, he was a graduate of the Army Computer Programmers Course at Fort Gordon, Georgia as an E4/Specialist. September 1992, he attended PLDC, at Fort McClellan. May 1996 to October 1999, he deployed to the United States Army Southern Command (USARSO) as a Systems Administrator at Fort Clayton and Fort Corozol, Panama during the transition of the Panama Canal to Panama. October 1998, he was promoted to E5/SGT and E6/SSG in 2000 with an assignment to 21st TSC in Kaiserslautern, Germany. November 2001, promoted to E7/SFC as the Information Technology NCO.

On March 2002, Mr. Levett was appointed as a Warrant Officer Candidate in the 122nd Corps Support Group (CSG). November 2002, he completed the Warrant Officer Candidate Course in Fort Rucker, with assignment to the CSSAMO of the 122nd CSG. August 2004, completed the Warrant Officer Basic Course at Fort Gordon. November 2004 to November 2005, he was deployed with the 122nd CSG to Ah Nasariya, Iraq as the CSSAMO Director and Deputy S6. Earned a Bronze Star Medal for exemplary work in Iraq. November 2004, promoted to CW2 by MG Allen Harrell. December 2005, he became the Network Manager at the JFHQ Alabama and promoted to CW3 in November 2008. May 2009, he became the Financial Systems Management Officer of Information Management Office. March of 2013, he became the Senior Protection Technician of Defensive

Cyberspace Operations at the JFHQ. December 2013, promoted to CW4. January 2014 to current, he serves as the Branch Chief for the Cyberspace Security Division for the AL-ARNG, earning a Meritorious Service Medal.

CW4 Levett continues to serve the United States Army and the Army National Guard with dignity, valor, honor, professionalism and selfless serve to help protect the rights and lives of the civilians of the United States of America.

Chief Warrant Officer Five Leonard R. Levy

Chief Warrant Officer Five Leonard R. Levy was born in Kingston, Jamaica. He migrated to the United States of America in March 1986, enlisted the Army in September 1986, and was accessed into the Warrant Officer Corps in December 1997. Chief Levy is currently assigned to the US Army Africa Command as the Materiel Readiness Chief/Senior Maintenance Advisor. To date, Chief Levy has over thirty one years of selfless service in defense of our Nation. He has been deployed in support of numerous operations to include Operation Enduring Freedom, Operation Iraqi Freedom, Operation Joint Endeavor, Operation Vigilant Warrior, and Operations Desert Shield and Storm. His previous assignments includes US Combined Arms Support Command, US Army Sustainment Command, Rock Island Arsenal, B Co, 115th BSB, 1st Cavalry Division, B Co, 2nd FSB, 2nd Infantry Division, and D Co, 4th FSB, 4th Infantry Division. As an enlisted Soldier, he served within 1st Armored Division, 24th Infantry Division, and the 2nd and 3rd Corps Support Commands. Chief Levy is an Ordnance Corps Branch warrant officer. His area of expertise is in both Armament Systems Maintenance and logistics operations.

Chief Warrant Officer Two Elvis Lee Mann

Spouse Name: ROCHELLE C. MANN
Rank, Branch, ARNGUS

Date and Place of Birth: MAY 19TH 1981, DURHAM, NC
Present Assignment: ARMAMENT WARRANT
Civilian Occupation: Electronics Supervisor (CSMS)
Enlisted Service: 12 YEARS
Source and Date of Commission: WARRANT, 15 NOV 12
Years of Active Commissioned Service: 2
Total Years of Service: 18

Military Schools Attended: Year Completed:
WOAC 2017
WOBC 2013
WOCC 2012
Indirect Fire Infantryman 2008
WLC 2007
Crane operator 2005
Small Arms Repairer 2005
Machinist 2001

Civilian Education: Diploma, South Granville High, some college Vance- Granville NC, Sonoran Desert Institute, AZ, Technical Management DeVry University, Morrisville NC
Degrees Received: A.S. Firearms Technology degree
B.S. Technical Management

U.S. Decorations and Badges: National Defense Service Medal, Global War on Terrorism Service Medal, Iraq Campaign Medal with campaign star, Army Service Ribbon, Overseas Service Ribbon, Armed Forces Reserve Medal with M device.

I was born in Durham, NC in 1981. I was raised in Creedmoor, NC. I got married in 2004 in Washington DC; I have two children boy and girl we enjoy fishing, hiking, outside work, and spending family time looking at movies. I come from a family of thirteen, which I was the youngest boy out of the thirteen. I worked on the family farm through the age of eight. When I was nine, my father died at the age of 61. My mother was left to raise five children on her own because the older children had moved out. By the time I was in middle school, my older brothers were a bad influence in my life. I had started to smoke and hang out late to fit in with my brothers.

In 1996, I just got in the eighth grade and had started to do better things in my life. I joined the wrestling team and was very successful at it. By me wrestling, I was always training and keeping busy. At the end of the wrestling season I was told that I ineligible to wrestling anymore, so I maintained a good spirit and continued doing well in school. Although I was not able to wrestling, I was there in the wrestling room with my teammates until the end of season.

In 1997, I attend South Granville High School, four years and graduated. While at South Granville, I joined JROTC my ninth grade year. While in JROTC, I learned leadership, team work, and being on the bottom of the totem pole. JROTC taught me a lot about being a leader and how to look out for the ones that is below rank. While in JROTC I did adopted-a-highway three time a month, instructed drill and ceremonies, and Silent Drill Team commander. I worked my way up the top by my senior year; I was the battalion XO and planned out the training schedule for the program.

Also, I joined the wrestling team my ninth grade year. My ninth grade year on the team, I was one of the best on the team. My coach saw a young man with great potential in wrestling. I wanted to start in the line-up that, so I had to wrestle off with a senior to get his spot at 135lbs. so, I did and kicked his butt. After that, I was praised for being young and for having so much fight. Throughout my high school wrestling career I accomplished many goals, by going to the North Carolina State Championships for three year and being in the top wrestler in the state. I got a letter from Oklahoma state to wrestle, but could not because I was the man around the house to take care of my mother and my two sisters. Also in high school I was in a honors show choir, we danced and singed for a grade, that was awesome considering the fact that I like to do both. I was always active in school to keep from getting into the wrong crowd.

Upon enlisting in the North Carolina National Guard, I was assigned to the Det.1 731st maintenance company located in Butner, North Carolina. I joined this unit in 2000 as an E-3; I started as an E-3 because of four years of JROTC in high. After doing six months in the 731st I was deployed to Fort Bragg under the 18th airborne corps in support of troops that was going overseas. After deployment I stayed with the unit for five years, and then moved to 691st maintenance company in Farmville, NC. While I was in 691st I became the unit armor for five years. I took an E-6 promotion in the Det. 1 694th maintenance company in Snow Hill, NC.

I start working at the Combine Support Maintenance Shop (CSMS) in 2003 as an allied trade helper, soon after I moved various jobs around the shop. I got a full-time job in the arms room in 2004 and became very skilled at repairing and inspecting weapons. I became the state inspector and currently still the state inspector for North Carolina National Guard.

Chief Warrant Officer Four Sharon M. Mullens

Chief Warrant Officer Four Sharon M. Mullens has had an astounding Army career that expands over three decades. Born in Annapolis, Maryland to a large naval family, Chief Mullens was no stranger to the military and the lifestyle it represented. She is an accomplished Senior Cyber Management Technician with Headquarters Military Intelligence Readiness Command with multiple Army Staff and operational assignments to include the United States Army Cyber Command and Headquarters, Department of the Army Pentagon. Her areas of assignment include Germany, Korea, Washington, DC, Fort Bragg, North Carolina and Fort Belvoir, Virginia. She has had multiple deployments in Operation Iraqi Freedom and Operation Enduring Freedom to include Kuwait, Qatar and Saudi Arabia. As the HHC Commander of Headquarters and Headquarters Detachment 335th Theatre Signal Command, Sharon was the first Black female warrant officer HHC Commander in a forward-deployed contingency operation.

Sharon graduated with a Bachelor's degree in Business Administration, with the honors of "magna cum laude" from Baker College of Flint, Michigan, to include a Master's in Business Administration. Her professional certifications are comprised of several information technology certifications, cyber skill identifiers, Warrant Officer Professional Military Education and Lean Six Sigma certifications. Her awards and decorations include the Bronze Star Medal, Meritorious Service Medal (4th OLC), Army Commendation Medal (3rd OLC), Joint Service Achievement Medal, Army Achievement Medal (3rd OLC), Army Good Conduct Medal (2nd OLC), the National Defense Service Medal, Southwest Asia Service

Medal, the Global War on Terrorism Service Medal, and the Global War on Terrorism Expeditionary Medal.

Chief Warrant Officer Five Aurelia "Viki" Murray (Retired)

Aurelia Victoria Murray was born in Columbus, Ohio. In 1966, she graduated from Marion-Franklin High School where she was a varsity cheerleader and member of the concert choir. Later that year,

she began her government service as a civilian employee with the Defense Construction Supply Center. Chief Murray continued her civilian government service at the Navy Finance Center, Cleveland, Ohio from 1970 until she was recruited by her father, then Senior Master Sergeant Thomas A. Murray, Sr. She enlisted with the 182nd Tactical Air Support Group, Illinois Air National Guard in June 1973 and began her career as a full-time technician.

In 1974, Chief Murray returned to Ohio and transferred to the 121st Combat Support Squadron, Ohio ANG. That year, she traded Air Force blue for Army green and became the first female to work as an Administrative Supply Technician in the Ohio Army National Guard. She was assigned to the 54th Support Center (Rear Area Operations) and later to the Headquarters Battery 136th Field Artillery Battalion where she attained the rank of Staff Sergeant.

In March 1978, Chief Murray became the second female and the first African-American female appointed to the Warrant Officer ranks in the Ohio National Guard. She was assigned as the Military Personnel Technician and full-time Command Administrative Specialist for Headquarters, 136th Field Artillery Battalion.

Chief Murray entered the Title 10, Active Guard Reserve (AGR) program in May 1982 with an assignment to the National Guard Professional Education Center (PEC) where she served as the Center's first female instructor. She remained at PEC until June of 1987, having served as a Training Support Writer for the last two years of that assignment. Her following assignment was at the Army Finance and Accounting Center, Indianapolis, Indiana, where she served as a Financial Assistance Officer in the National Guard Financial Services Office.

At the rank of CW3, Chief Murray was recalled to her home state in July 1988 to serve as the State Recruiting and Retention Specialist where she remained until returning to the Title 10, AGR Program. In March 1993, she reported for duty at the National Guard Bureau (NGB), Personnel Division, where she was promoted to CW4 and served as a Military Personnel Technician in the SIDPERS branch. She was assigned to the NGB Policy, Programs and Manpower Division, in 1995 and in December 1998 became the first woman to serve as the ARNG Warrant Officer Program Manager.

In September 1999, Chief Murray became the first African-American female in the history of the Army to be promoted to the rank of Chief Warrant Officer Five.

CW5 Murray was assigned to the Office of the Deputy Chief of Staff for National Guard, U.S. Army Forces Command from May 2001 until September 2003. She was then assigned to Headquarters, Department of the Army, Office of the Deputy Chief of Staff, Personnel (G-1) at the Pentagon from September 2003 until May 2005. Her 33-year career culminated with her assignment to the NGB-J5, Plans and Policy Division where she served as Policy Analyst and Policy Branch Chief.

Chief Murray is currently a graduate student pursuing her Master Degree. She holds a bachelor's degree in social psychology from Park University, where she graduated magna cum laude in 1998. Her military awards include the Meritorious Service Medal (3 awards), Army Commendation Medal (4 awards), Army Achievement Medal (2 awards), National Defense Service Medal (2 awards), the Humanitarian Service Medal, and the Global War on Terrorism Service Medal

Chief Warrant Officer Five Alfred J. Myles US Army, Retired (Deceased)
US Military Intelligence Hall of Fame

CW5 Alfred Myles entered the Army in July 1971 and completed basic training at Fort Polk, Louisiana. In 1974, then SPC Myles attended Imagery Intelligence Analyst training at Fort Huachuca, Arizona, and was assigned to Company A, 1st MI Battalion at Fort Bragg, North Carolina. While at Fort Bragg, he became the Noncommissioned Officer-in-Charge (NCOIC) of the Imagery Section with the US Forces Command Mobile Training Detachment, which trained Active, Reserve and National Guard units on military intelligence tactics, techniques, and procedures. In 1978, SSG Myles was assigned to the Doctrine Development Division at Fort Huachuca, where he wrote the Army correspondence course and Skill Qualification Test (SQT) for Imagery Intelligence Analysts. In February 1981, SSG Myles was directly appointed to Warrant Officer One and assigned to the Intelligence, Threat and Analysis Center (ITAC) in Washington, DC. During his time at ITAC, Chief Myles was a major contributor to the discovery of the new Soviet main battle tank (T-80).

In 1983, CW5 Myles was assigned to the Imagery Detachment, 470th MI Group, at Fort Clayton, Panama. During this assignment, he spearheaded the imagery support to the US Embassies, US Southern Command and its allies in Central and South America. He was instrumental in developing imagery signatures to identify insurgent and drug trafficking activities. He also coordinated the layout of a giant mosaic to support the security efforts for the El Salvadorian Peace Talks in 1984. Later in 1997, as a Chief Warrant Officer Four, he was assigned to the MI Warrant Officer Training Branch as Course Manager for the Imagery Intelligence Technician Certification Course.

In 1998, CW5 Myles became the Imagery Advisor to the Saudi Arabian Intelligence School in Al Khaj, Saudi Arabia, where he spearheaded the development of an Imagery Advance Course and taught the Saudi Arabian cadre how to teach this course. In 2000, he became the first Imagery Intelligence Warrant Officer to achieve the rank of Chief Warrant Officer Five, the highest rank a Warrant Officer can achieve.

CW5 Myles completed his 33-year Army career at Fort Huachuca while assigned as the Chief, Warrant Officer Training Branch, where he was a major contributor to the Warrant Officer training and development programs and Officer Education System. He earned numerous military awards during his career including the Defense Meritorious Service

Medal, Meritorious Service Medal (4 Oak Leaf Clusters), Army Commendation Medal (2 Oak Leaf Clusters), and the Army Achievement Medal (1 Oak Leaf Cluster).

CW5 Myles was inducted into the MI Hall of Fame in 2011. He passed away in 2013.

Chief Warrant Officer Five (Retired) Ray M. Noble

CW5 Ray M. Noble is a native of Savannah, Georgia and was born on January 30, 1954. He entered the Army on August 24, 1973. He attended Basic Training and Advanced Individual Training at Fort Jackson, South Carolina and Fort Knox, Kentucky. An eleven year enlisted career followed with him serving in positions of increasing responsibility as tracked vehicle repairman, foreman, section chief, and maintenance sergeant in the United States and in Germany. In 1984, Sergeant First Class Noble received his appointment as a Warrant Officer.

Mr. Noble's initial assignment as a Warrant Officer from 1984 to 1987 was as an automotive maintenance technician in the 5th Infantry Division, 3rd Squadron, 12th U.S. Calvary, Fort Polk, Louisiana. From there, he was assigned to the 3rd Armored Division, 8th Battalion, 3rd Calvary, Gelnhausen, Germany from 1988 to 1991 as the Battalion maintenance technician, where he deployed in support of Operations Desert Shield / Desert Storm. Remaining in Germany, his next assignment was with the 2nd Armored Division, 3rd Battalion, 66th Armor, Garkstadt, Germany from 1991 to 1992. From 1992 to 1994, CW5 Noble served as the support staff maintenance officer for the 5th Combat Equipment Support Battalion West, Combat Company, Primasens, Germany. He returned to the United States and was assigned to the 1st Calvary Division, Fort Hood, Texas with duties in Mississippi in support of the 155th Armor Brigade as a maintenance advisor and resident trainer form 1994 to 1997. From 1997 to 2001, he was assigned to Fort Stewart, Georgia, 3rd Infantry Division, 3rd Squadron, 7th U.S. Calvary as a staff maintenance officer where he deployed to Kuwait in support of Operation Intrinsic Action. From

2001 to 2004, he served as the logistics management officer for the 2nd Corps Support Command Materiel Management Center, Equipment Readiness Division, Fort Bragg, North Carolina. In 2004, Mr. Noble went to support the 2nd Infantry Division, Division Support Command and Camp Casey, Republic of Korea from 2004 to 2005 as the logistics management officer. He then reported to Fort Stewart, Georgia from 2005 to 2007, serving in the 3rd Infantry Division, Division Support Command as the logistics management officer.

CW5 Ray Noble served the United States Army for 40 years, prior to retiring as the senior ordnance logistics officer for 3rd Infantry Division, G4 Ground Maintenance Section with five combat tours in support of Operations Desert Shield and Desert Storm, Operation Iraqi Freedom, Operation New Dawn and Operation Enduring Freedom.

Mr. Noble's military education includes Warrant Officers Basic Course, Advanced Course, Warrant Officer Intermediate Level Education Course, and the Warrant Officer Senior Education Course. The rest of his military education includes Army Maintenance Management Course, Logistics Management Development Course, Defense Distribution Management Course from the US Army Logistics Management College, Contracting Officer's Representative Course from the Defense Acquisition University and Airborne School. He received an Associate's degree in Automotive Service from Central Texas College, and a Bachelor of Degree in Business Administration from Northwestern State University, Louisiana. He holds Automotive Service Excellence Certifications and is Six Sigma Lean, Green Belt Certified.

His awards and decorations include: the Legion of Merit, Bronze Star Medal (4olc), Meritorious Service Medal (7olc), Army Commendation Medal (3olc), Army Achievement Medal (5olc), Good Conduct Medal (3rd award), National Defense Service Medal (3rd award), Armed Forces Expeditionary Medal, South West Asian Medal (3 campaign stars), Afghanistan Campaign Medal, Iraq Campaign Medal (6 campaign stars), Global War on Terrorism Expeditionary Medal (1 campaign star), Global War on Terrorism Service Medal, Korean Defense Service Medal, NCO Professional Development Ribbon, Amy Service Ribbon, Overseas Service Ribbon (10th award),

NATO Medal, Kuwait Liberation Medal Saudi (sa), Kuwait Liberation Medal Kuwait (ku), Valorous Unit Award, Meritorious Unit Citation (2nd award), Parachutist Badge, and the Mechanic Badge.

CW5 Noble is the recipient of the Ordnance Corps Order of Samuel Sharp and the US Cavalry & Armor Association Noble Patron of Armor Award. He is an active Life Member of the U.S. Army Ordnance Corps and the U.S. Army Warrant Officers Association, (Marne Chapter), the Veterans of Foreign Wars and the American Legion.

Appointment ceremony to Warrant Officer at
Aberdeen Proving Grounds, Maryland 24 April 1984.

Promotion ceremony to CW5 at Fort Stewart,
Georgia on 1 February 2001 with wife Brenda.

Warrant Officer One Olutayo A. (Ty) Ogundare

I was born in Ile-Ife, Oyo State (now Osun State) Nigeria, West Africa in the early 70s. I received my Bachelor's Degree from Obafemi Awolowo University in Nigeria with a major in English Language and a minor in Literature. Upon settling down in the United States, I went back to school and received a Diploma in Paralegal Studies in 2000; completed my Master's degree in 2006 with a major in Public Administration at Hamline University, St. Paul, Minnesota.

I enlisted in the Army National Guard in 2003 with the ultimate goal of becoming a Warrant Officer. As an enlisted Soldier, I have had opportunities as an M-day Soldier to work in various units ranging from Infantry, Signal, Chemical, Aviation and Human Resources Companies.

In 2008, I was deployed to Iraq for a year. My experience in Iraq gave me the push to redefine my life and set goals to make a positive changes in my military career and in the society and aspire to be a "clean cut" Officer. Upon returning from deployment, I moved to the East Coast from the Upper Midwest to continue my National Guard career with the Delaware Army National Guard and pursue my goal of becoming a Warrant Officer.

Presently, I am working fulltime as a Security Specialist at the Joint Force Headquarters in New Castle, Delaware functioning as the State Personnel Security Manager/State Awards Administrator/Government Passport Agent and as a Human Resources Officer on the M-Day side.

Chief Warrant Officer Four (Retired) Preston Oliver

Chief Warrant Officer Four Preston Oliver (retired), enlisted in the Florida Army National Guard on March 9, 1964. After attending Basic Training at Fort Dix New Jersey, he was assigned to 337th Signal Depot in Jacksonville, Florida. In 1968, he transferred to Headquarters Company, 146th Signal Battalion where he served in several leadership positions. In 1972, Chief Warrant Officer Four Oliver was assigned to the 853rd Supply and Service Company as a Platoon Sergeant. A year later, he was promoted to First Sergeant and continued to serve in the 853rd.

Mr. Oliver would later obtain the rank of Warrant Officer Two in 1984 and Chief Warrant Officer Three in 1990. He transferred to Headquarters Detachment, Camp Blanding Joint Training Center as Property Accountant Technician and was promoted in 1995 to Chief Warrant Officer Four.

Chief Warrant Officer Four Oliver continued his service until his retirement in 2005. He served in the Florida Army National Guard for 41 years, 3 months and four days.

Chief Warrant Officer Oliver was activated several times to assist residence through the state of Florida when hurricane related incidents struck the peninsula. His professionalism, leadership and direct guidance made it possible for the Florida Army National Guard to complete its dedicated missions.

His awards and decorations include the Meritorious Service Medal, Army Commendation Medal, Army Achievement Medal, Army Reserve Component Medal 9th Award, National Defense Service Medal with Bronze Star, Humanitarian Service Medal, Army Forces Reserved Medal 4th Award, Army Service Ribbon, Army Reserve Component Training Ribbon Numeral 4, Florida Service Medal 2nd

Award, Florida Commendation Medal 6th Award, Florida Meritorious Service Ribbon 5th Award, Florida Service Ribbon 8th Award and the Florida Active State Duty Ribbon 6th Award.

While in the Florida Army National Guard, he served as Community Involvement Vice President with the Jacksonville Jaycees from 1973-1976. He volunteered his time to mentor young people to excel in the areas of business development, management skills, individual training and networking through various community service and social gatherings. Preston Oliver was recognized several times for his dedicated commitment and received the Jacksonville Jaycees Man of the Quarter award and the Robert L. Shirmer Award (Jaycee of the Year).

On September 29, 1996, Preston Oliver was ordained as a Deacon at Shiloh Metropolitan Baptist Church in Jacksonville, Fl. As a Deacon, he's been recognized several times for his loyalty, dedication and commitment to the church, its member and the community.

Preston Oliver also committed his time with helping the Alpha Kappa Alpha Sorority Inc. with several community service events and social gatherings. Due to his unwavering commitment, Alpha Kappa Alpha Sorority Inc., was recognized several for their achievement for helping the community.

Due to his actions, Preston Oliver was presented a Helping Hands Community Service Award on February 16, 2008 from the Phi Eta Omega Chapter, Alpha Kappa Alpha Sorority Inc.

Chief Warrant Officer Two Michael Philbert

Michael Philbert was born in Brooklyn New York to Mortimer Philbert and Paula Benjamin. In school high school he loved to wear dress clothes every day so he earned the nick name "Church Boy". He joined the Army in 2003 as an Information Systems Operator and attended basic training at Fort Benning Georgia. After Advanced Individual Training at Fort Gordon, he boarded his first flight to start his journey on active duty in Stuttgart Germany with the 52nd Signal Battalion. In 2005, he received orders to report to the top of the Signal Corps food chain, NETCOM. Enthusiastically he reported later that year only to receive the "it's not you, it's me talk" as his gaining unit broke the news that there were no slots for Soldiers of his rank and they had kindly arranged for him to report to a local Signal unit that would be deploying soon. As a good Soldier, he reported to the 86th Signal Battalion in Fort Huachuca Arizona where he became the Post Soldier of the year before deploying to Iraq.

While deployed, Philbert achieved the rank of Sergeant and was nominated to serve on the Multi-National Forces Iraq Commanding General's Communications Team providing personal communication support to GEN David Petraeus. He travelled throughout Iraq observing infrastructure development and engagements with foreign leaders that were shaping the future of the country. Following his deployment, he returned to United States Army Europe (USAREUR) where he supported GEN Carter Ham as he headed the work group tasked with the repeal of the "Don't Ask, Don't Tell" policy. In 2011 until 2012, he toured Europe with LTG Mark Hertling helping to deliver the strategic message of USAREUR and strengthening partnerships with our NATO allies.

In 2012, he was selected to join the Warrant Officer Cohort. His first assignment was as the Group S6 for the Criminal Investigation Division in Savannah Georgia. He introduced tablet technology to the organization and demonstrated how they could be used to streamline investigative operations. In 2016, Mr. Philbert returned to USAREUR as the Officer in Charge of the Commanding General's Communications Team where he influenced strategic direction by shaping policy, implementing emerging technologies, and helping to build interoperability with coalition partners to deter Russian aggression throughout Europe. During his third tour in Europe, he completed his Associates in Management Studies and Bachelor in Cyber Security Management and Policies.

Mr. Philbert's passion for mentorship led him to create an organization named Military Mentor aimed at aligning leaders of the U.S. Armed Forces with youth that are seeking lifelong mentorship. There is a systemic accountability problem throughout America that has resulted in our youth not receiving the leadership they require to make better and more informed decisions. As a result, there is increased crime, drug use and suicides rates complemented with decreased high school graduation and productivity of kids primarily in low income communities. Mr. Philbert believes that the leadership training, experience and skills of Military leaders can be leveraged to the benefit of our youth by providing alternative leadership options outside of the poor ones they tend to follow in their communities. He firmly believes that the execution of the commitment to our nation starts at home, not abroad.

CW2 Michael Philbert and his wife
Selena attending a reception during
Warrant Officer Basic Course. This
was the first formal event they attended
together since he made his transition
into the Cohort. She has been his
backbone since he was an E-5 aspiring
to become a Warrant Officer.

CHIEF WARRANT OFFICER FOUR KEITH R. PRATHER
Deputy Command Chief Warrant Officer of the U.S. Army Reserve Legal Command

Chief Warrant Officer Four (CW4) Keith R. Prather is a 40 year Army veteran currently serving as the Deputy Command Chief Warrant Officer (CCWO) and the Sexual Harassment/Assault Response Program Manager for the U.S. Army Reserve Legal Command in Gaithersburg, MD.

His previous assignments include: Senior Legal Administrator for the Office of the Staff Judge Advocate at the 99th Regional Support Command; Joint Base McGuire, Dix, Lakehurst, NJ; Senior Legal Administrator, 213th Legal Operations Detachment, Decatur, GA; Public Affairs Officer, 2145th Garrison Support Unit, Baghdad, Iraq; Commander, 2145th Provisional Holding Company, Fort Benning, GA; Executive Officer, 678th Personnel Services Company, Nashville, TN; Senior Legal Administrator, 139th Legal Operations Detachment, Nashville, TN.

CW4 Prather is a graduate of the Warrant Officer Senior Staff Course, Warrant Officer Staff Course, and the JAG Warrant Officer Advanced and Basic Courses, AG Warrant Officer Basic Course, DoD Mediation Course, DoD Equal Opportunity Advisors Course, DoD Public Affairs Course (BJC and PA Supervisor),and the Army Facilitator Certification Course.

His awards include the Meritorious Service Medal (with 2 Oak Leaf Clusters); Army Commendation Medal (with 3 Oak Leaf Clusters); Army Achievement Medal (with 1 Oak Leaf Cluster); Army Reserve Component Achievement Medal (with 2 Oak Leaf Clusters); National Defense Service Medal (with Bronze Star); Southwest Asia

Service Medal (with Bonze Service Star); Armed Forces Reserve Medal (with "M" Device and Gold Hour Glass); NCO Professional Development Ribbon (with Numeral 3) and the Army Service Ribbon.

CW4 Prather holds a Master of Science Degree in Human Services-Non-Profit Management from Murray State University, and a Bachelor of Science Degree in Public Management from Austin Peay State University.

Chief Warrant Officer Four Jean D. Ritter

Chief Warrant Officer Four Jean D. Ritter was born in the Bronx in New York City. She was raised in the Upper West Side of Manhattan by her adopted mother who was already raising two other children of her own – her sister Karen was 7 being the youngest of three, Jean, thrived. She was raised in the same New York City housing project, Dyckman Projects, and attended the same Catholic School, St. Jude, as Lou Alcindor a.k.a. Kareem Abdul Jabbar. Growing up in a New York City project was fun and different. Jean was an exceptional child – while attending St. Jude School, her mother was asked if Jean could be skipped because she was a gifted child. Concerned for her wellbeing, Jean's mother refused. At the end of Jean's fifth grade school year, her mother, now a single parent, asked Jean if she would like to attend public school.

Understanding the probable financial strain her mother was experiencing and wanting to be with her friends, Jean gladly agreed to attend public school. At the start of the school year, her mom was again asked about Jean being skipped to a higher grade and again she refused. She wanted Jean to remain with her peers. It wasn't until Jean made it to middle school, seventh grade, and was able to skip the high school after successfully completing a rigorous curriculum covering seventh and eighth grade work. All of this time, Jean was the youngest of her class and graduated John F. Kennedy High School in the Bronx in 1986 at the tender age of 16 before becoming a college freshman at Kutztown University in Pennsylvania.

Jean did not complete her college education at that time; instead she went on to work and started a family before joining the Army in 1998. As a Private Second Class, Jean attended Basic at Fort Jackson, South Carolina and the Advanced Individual Training at Fort Lee, Virginia to become an Automated Logistical Specialist. Her first duty station was Fort Lewis, Washington in 1999. Jean served as part of the 24th Quartermaster (QM) Supply Company Direct Support in the supply warehouse. During her two years at 24th QM, Jean experienced much success as a soldier. She earned recognition for being the Soldier of the Month and Quarter before relocating to her next duty station at Camp Casey, Korea.

During Jean's time at Camp Casey, she served with distinction in the Division Support Command, Materiel Management Office as the Automated Processing Department specialist responsible for ensuring successful completion of the automated supply processes. In 2002, Jean relocated again, this time to Fort Bragg, North Carolina. At Bragg, Jean served as the Repair Parts Specialist for the 189th Combat Support Battalion responsible for ordering repair parts for the equipment for the battalion. Jean was promoted to Sergeant and deployed with the 189th to Iraq in early 2003 and again in late 2004. During her first deployment, Jean again displayed excellence, by competing and winning battalion Non-Commissioned Officer of the Year. It was during her second deployment that Jean decided she wanted to become a Warrant Officer. In August 2006, Jean successfully completed Warrant Officer Candidate School at Fort Rucker, Alabama and then graduated Warrant Officer Basic Course at Fort Lee, Virginia – officially becoming a Supply Systems Technician.

Warrant Officer One Jean Ritter's position was as the Accountable Officer of Supply Point 51 located at Yongsan, Korea for the 595th Maintenance Company. During her two years as the accountable officer, Jean again experienced success by winning numerous supply excellence awards at the local and Army-wide levels. Her last year in Korea, as a Warrant Officer Two, Jean worked as the Senior Supply Systems Technician in the 498th Combat Sustainment Support Battalion Support Operations Office. Jean was directly responsible for managing two warehouses and both warehouses won numerous local and Army-wide supply excellence awards. In late 2010, Jean competed and won the chance to represent Eighth Army Army-wide in the Douglas MacArthur Leadership Award competition on her way to 3rd Sustainment Command (Expeditionary) at Fort Knox, Kentucky.

While serving as the Senior Supply Systems Technician, Materiel Management Officer, in the Support Operations Section, Jean deployed to Afghanistan in 2012. For nine months, Jean was responsible for at least 18 supply support activities (SSA) and was instrumental in the planning of the drawdown for the SSAs. A few months after redeploying back to Fort Knox, Jean was selected to participate in the Training with Industry program in Cadillac, Michigan at AAR Mobility Systems. This program allows select Army personnel to train and work in the private sector for twelve months with a utilization tour at Fort Lee, Virginia. Jean arrived at Fort Lee, Virginia in October of 2014 and served as a Capabilities Developer. She continued to have success both professionally and personally before relocating to Fort Leavenworth, Kansas where she is now a Chief Warrant Officer Four with a Master's Degree in International Management and serving as an Instructor/Writer at the Army Management Staff College, Organizational Leadership department.

CW4 Ritter's awards and decorations include the Bronze Star Medal, Meritorious Service Medal, Army Commendation Medal (5), Army Achievement (3) Medal, Army Good Conduct Medal (2), National Defense Service Medal, Afghanistan Campaign Medal, Iraq Campaign Medal (2), Global War on Terrorism Expeditionary and Service Medals, Korean Defense Service Medal, Non-Commissioned Officer Professional Development Ribbon (2), Army Service Ribbon, Overseas Ribbon (6), Meritorious Unit Commendation Ribbon, and Combat Action Badge.

My Journey By Chief Warrant Officer Four Vickie Slade

My Journey to becoming a warrant officer began 09 February 1979 when I enlisted in the US Army Reserve at the young and naïve age of 18.

My career as a Soldier and Warrant Officer was made possible because of the remarkable people God placed along my path. From the Sergeant in basic training, who after two weeks of seeing me cry every day, told me that I really needed to stop crying (I cried when the Soldier standing next to me got yelled at), to the Sergeant in Advanced Individual Training (AIT) who told me that just because there was snow on the ground *in early September*, did not mean I could sleep in and miss formation (stop laughing), to all the mentors who encouraged and supported my endeavor to become a warrant officer, and last but certainly not least, to CW5 Sharon Swartworth, my friend and catalyst for my accession onto active duty.

Whenever I'm asked why or how I came to join the military, I tell the story about the day I was at work on my part-time job as a clerk typist for the Social Security Administration. On that day, 08 February 1979, I was proof reading a document when I heard a commotion about 50 feet from my desk. Curiosity got the best of me, so I walked over to the desk where several people were laughing and talking. I asked the young lady sitting at the desk what all the excitement was about. She said, "I just joined the CAS program in the military. I thought this CAS program must really be something if she's this excited. She told me that CAS was an acronym for Civilian Acquired Skills and gave me her recruiter's name and number. I walked back to my desk and immediately called the recruiter. He told me I did not meet the perquisites for the CAS program but that he would be glad to talk to me about other military options. The recruiter picked me up from my house at 0600 hours the next morning and drove me to the recruiting station. We discussed the Reserve Program and Active Duty. I liked the idea of drilling one weekend a month and attending annual training two weeks during the summer. After completing some paperwork, the recruiter took me to the Military Entrance Processing Station (MEPS). At 1500 hours on that same day, I was sworn into the US Army Reserve's Delayed Entry Program as a Private E-1.

I've had many amazing experiences and opportunities since joining the military; I served in all of the Army's components (Reserve, Active Duty, and National Guard); I was the first Legal Engagements Warrant Officer in the Department of Defense; and I jumped out of perfectly good airplanes.

As I look back on that day in February 1979, I was exactly where I was supposed to be and 38 years later I'm a Warrant Officer in the United States Army National Guard, which is exactly where I'm supposed to be. HOOAH!

Picture taken on 2 Aug 17 at Davidson Army Airfield, Fort Belvoir, Virginia. CW4 Slade was one of several volunteers to accompany the DC Army National Guard during a professional development training flight over Washington, DC.

Chief Warrant Officer Five Joel D. Smith

Chief Warrant Officer Five Joel D. Smith was born on Fort Campbell, Kentucky. He is currently serving as a Detailed Inspector General within the Office of The Inspector General, Department of the Army.

He entered the Army National Guard in 1983. During his tenure as an enlisted Soldier in the Guard, he served as a Medical Specialist. He entered active duty in 1988 and attended the Initial Entry Rotary Wing flight training.

As an Army Aviator, CW5 Smith has served four tours in the Republic of Korea with the 17th Aviation Brigade, 6th U.S. Calvary (CAB), 3rd Military Intelligence Aerial Exploitation Battalion; with 11th Aviation Regiment, Germany; with 82nd Combat Aviation Brigade and 229th Aviation Regiment, Fort Bragg, North Carolina; and 4th Combat Aviation Brigade and Task Force ODIN-Afghanistan, Fort Hood, Texas.

He previously served with Human Resources Command as its first Command Chief Warrant Officer in Fort Knox, Kentucky. He additionally served within HRC as the AH-64A/D Career Manager in Alexandria, Virginia. Another human resources assignment saw CW5 Smith served as the Warrant Officer Strength Manager, Colonel's Manager and Assistant General Officer Manager for Army Forces Command (FORSCOM), Fort McPherson, Georgia.

His combat tours include serving as the Senior Warrant Officer, Master Gunner and Tactical Operations Officer for Task Force Odin-Afghanistan, and as AH-64D Standardization Officer within the 101st, 159th, 3rd and 10th Combat Aviation Brigades.

CW5 Smith is qualified through the Fixed-Wing Qualification Course, EO-7 and Medium Altitude Reconnaissance and Surveillance

System courses, AH-64A/D Aircraft Qualification Course, Rotary Wing Instrument Flight Examiner Course, Master Gunner Course, Tactical Operations Course, OH-58A/C and AH-64A/D Instructor Pilot Course.

CW5 Smith is a graduate of the Warrant Officer Advance, Staff and Senior Staff Courses. He is presently completing a Master of Science in Leadership and holds a Bachelor of Science degree in Aerospace. He is also Green and Black Belt certified for Lean Six Sigma certification.

His awards include the Combat Action Badge, Master Army Aviator Badge, Air Assault Badge, Legion of Merit, Bronze Star Medal, Meritorious Service Medal with silver oak leaf, Air Medal, Army Commendation Medal with four oak leaf clusters, Army Achievement Medal with two oak leaf clusters, National Defense Service Medal with second award and the NATO Medal with third award.

Chief Warrant Officer Four Ramon Taylor

CW4 Ramon Taylor is a United States Army Reserve Soldier who has served over 26 years, with three combat tours in 2003, 2008 and 2011. During his 2003 tour with the 751st QM Co, in support of Operation Enduring Freedom and later Operation Iraqi Freedom, Mr. Taylor (then WO1 Taylor) along with his warehouse platoon, setup the Army's first ever Capture Enemy Equipment warehouses/support activity. Their mission was to the consolidation and storage of all capture Iraqi multi-class warehouses, and theater-wide capture weapons, and establish a CEM SSA to re-issue the weapons and Class II to the U.S. Forces and Multi-National Forces in support of the Iraqi Army and the Iraqi Civil Defense Corps (ICDC).

Working with U.S. and Multi-National Forces, CW4 Taylor and his warehouse platoon of 22 Soldiers, consolidated 55 captured Iraqi warehouse to 22 warehouses and managed over 1,000,000 pieces of captured Class II, Class VII (U.S. Sherman tank) and over 48

thousands captured weapons from various countries (Korea, German, Soviet Union, U.S., and more).

CW4 Taylor and his Soldiers helped outfit over 7 Battalions of the newly formed Iraqi Civil Defense Corp (ICDC). This was accomplished by CW4 Taylor development of a Microsoft Access database application to perform the automation of issue, receipt, storage and inventory of the captured equipment.

Chief Warrant Officer Four (Retired) John Thomas Tims

CW4 John T. Tims was born August 1, 1947 in Clover South Carolina. He was drafted and entered the Army June of 1968. He completed basic training at Fort Bragg NC and Advance Individual Training at Fort Eustis VA. He served as a 61A Seaman and boat operator, 535th Engineer Detachment (Floating Power Plant) (Nuclear) at Fort Davis Canal Zone. During a break in service, 1971 to 1977, he served in the Reserves / National Guards. He reenlisted into the Army in November 1977.

Mr. Tims completed his AIT at Fort Lee VA as a 76D, and was assigned as a PLL/TAMMS Clerk and NCOIC of the consolidated PLL/TAMMS clerks in the 317th Engineers in West Germany. He then served as a Drill Sergeant at Fort Dix NJ. He applied and received approval orders in May of 1989 to attend Warrant Officers Candidate School, at Fort Rucker AL. He received his appointment to W01 September 1989 at Fort Lee VA.

Mr. Tims' assignments as a Warrant Officer included, Fort Lewis Washington, 709th Infantry Missile Supply Support Activity; West Germany, 927th Aviation Battalion; Bosnia and Herzegovina (Joint Endeavor), 127th AVN; the 82nd Air Borne Division, Fort Bragg; 2nd Support Center Automated Service Division, Fort Bragg, North Carolina; Sinai, the Multi National Force & Observers; and the US Embassy, Manama Bahrain.

His Military awards include the Legion of Merit, The Meritorious Service Medal (5th award) Army Commendation Medal (5th Award) Army Achievement Medal (2nd award) Army Good Conduct Medal (4th Award) National Defense Service Medal (3rd award) Armed Forces Service Medal Noncommissioned Officer's Professional

Development Ribbon (w/Numeral 3) Army Service Ribbon Overseas Ribbon &7th Award) Drill Sergeant Identification Badge.

CW4 John T. Tims (Retired February 1, 2005) distinguished himself by exceptionally meritorious service in positions of great trust and responsibility throughout a stellar career spanning 33 years of service.

Chief Warrant Officer Four Anthony Thompson

Chief Thompson joined the United States Army through the delayed entry program on July 3, 1985, as a junior in high school. He graduated in the top 10% of his high school class from Deerfield Beach High School in Deerfield Beach, Florida in June of 1986. Chief Thompson entered basic training just 9 days later on June 26, 1986 at Fort Leonard Wood, Missouri. He was the Distinguished Honor Graduate of his Advance Individual Training class at Fort Lee, Virginia for the MOS of 76V (Material Handling Specialist).

Mr. Thompson reported to his first duty station on (31 October 1986-89), at Fort Hood, Texas. He then went overseas to serve at Camp Humphries, Korea (Oct 1989-90) and then on to Fort Riley, Kansas (Oct 1990- Mar 92).

Chief Thompson has served in two wars; Persian Gulf War ('91) and Operation Iraqi Freedom ('03-04). After an honorable discharge from active duty Chief Thompson joined the Florida National Guard in April 1992. Chief Thompson played a major role in Humanitarian efforts for Hurricane Andrew (Aug 1992). During Operation Iraqi freedom Chief Thompson and his platoon established a Class IX warehouse from the ground up with over 3200 lines and a value well over 3 million dollars.

Chief Thompson is now with the 260th Military Intelligence Battalion in Miami, Florida where they just provided supported the state for Hurricane Irma (Sep 2017). This is Chief Thompson's 12th State active duty mission to date.

Chief Warrant Officer Five James C. Tolbert, Retired

Mr. Jim Tolbert retired from Active Duty on 1 November 2005 culminating a 32-year career. In his final military assignment, he served as the 8th Regimental Chief Warrant Officer, United States Army Quartermaster School/Corps. He currently serves as the Deputy Chief for the Office of the Quartermaster General, United States Army Quartermaster School.

Chief Warrant Officer Five Tolbert received his Warrant Officer appointment after completing the Warrant Officer Candidate Course at Fort Rucker. Throughout his Warrant Officer career, he served in a variety of career enhancing assignments that includes Battalion Supply Technician, 223rd Aviation Battalion; Property Book Officer, 26th Signal Battalion, during this assignment he deployed to Saudi Arabia in support of both "Operations Desert Shield and Desert Storm"; Property Book Team Chief and later Chief Asset Visibility Section, Division Materiel Management Center, 4th Infantry Division, Fort Carson; Property Book Officer, United States Army Central Command-Forward, Camp Doha, Kuwait; Instructor United States Army Quartermaster Center and School; Personnel Career Management Officer, United States Total Army Personnel Command.

CW5 Tolbert completed every level of the Warrant Officer Education System which includes the Warrant Officer Candidate Course, Supply and Service Management Officer Course, Standard Property Book System Course, Corps Supply Staff Officer Course, Warrant Officer Advance Course, Contracting Officer Representative Course, the Warrant Officer Staff Course, The Army's Force Management Course, and the Warrant Officer Senior Staff Course. He holds a Master's Degree in Logistics Systems Management from Colorado Technical University at Colorado Springs, Colorado.

CW5 Tolbert is authorized to wear the Legion of Merit, Bronze Star Medal, Meritorious Service Medal (with 6 Oak Leaf Clusters), Army Commendation Medal (2 OLC), Army Achievement Medal (5 OLC), National Defense Service Medal with Bronze Stars, Southwest Asia Medal with Bronze Star, Armed Forces Expeditionary Medal, Saudi/Kuwait Liberation Medal, and the Kuwait Liberation Medal.

CW5 Tolbert is a 2009 Quartermaster Hall of Fame Inductee and a recipient of the Distinguished Order of Saint Martin.

Chief Warrant Officer Four Keisha D. Towles

Keisha Dornailla Towles (Apr. 18, 1975-) is the first African American woman selected to serve as the Proponent Chief and the first African American to serve as the Senior Signal Warrant Officer Assignment Officer for Signal Branch. Keisha was also on the team that created the Cyber Branch and developed the Warrant Officer Military Occupation Specialty (MOS) 170A, Cyber Operations Technician.

Keisha D. Towles was born in Fort Smith, Arkansas. She enlisted into the U.S. Army Reserves in 1993 and attended Basic Training at Fort Leonard Wood, Missouri and the Chaplain's Assistant Course at Fort Monmouth, New Jersey. She then enlisted on active duty in 1994 and attended the Information Systems Operator Course at Fort Gordon, Georgia. She was appointed as an Army Warrant Officer in 2002 and attended the Information Systems Warrant Officer Basic Course at Fort Gordon, Georgia.

CW4 Towles has deployed in support of Operation Iraqi Freedom (OIF) I, Baghdad, Iraq; Task Force Hurricane Katrina, New Orleans, Louisiana; OIF 06-08, Baghdad, Iraq; and Operation New Dawn and Operation Enduring Freedom Camp Airfjan, Kuwait.

Ms. Towles graduated from University of Maryland University College with a Bachelor of Science Degree in Computer Studies. She has also earned her Master of Science Degree in Information Technology Management with an emphasis in Business Intelligence from Trident University International. SFC Pernell Towles, Jr. from Abbeville, Louisiana married Keisha in 1999 and they have one son name Keeshon.

CW4 Towles was recently selected for promotion to CW5 and continues to serve in the Army as a passionate, tough, charismatic technical leader.

Brenda J.S. (Phillips) Payne White

My name is Brenda J.S. (Phillips) Payne White and I served on active duty in the Army and Desert Storm and I served on active duty in the Army National Guard. I am originally from the state of Georgia. I grew up in a family with eleven other siblings and my parents were sharecroppers in rural Georgia. I was the only one out of twelve that joined the military.

I graduated from Kentucky State University with a Bachelor's degree in Social Work and a minor in Gerontology and I later acquired an Associate's Degree in Paralegal Studies and became a certified Kentucky paralegal.

I am currently the business owner of Bluegrass Signing Agent and Consulting LLC where I operate as an independent Contractor for real estate, title and escrow companies and a fulltime notary public for the state of Kentucky and have been active for over five years.

I try to wake up every day with an open mind and an opportunity to network to expand my business revenue.

Chief Warrant Officer Four Curtis Wilson

Chief Warrant Officer 4 Curtis Wilson, United States Army, Ohio Army National Guard, for 37 years distinguished himself by exceptional meritorious conduct in the performance of outstanding service to the United States as Senior Ordnance Ground Maintenance Warrant Officer for the Joint Forces Head Quarters of the Ohio Army National Guard. CW4 Wilson has been instrumental to the State both technically and tactically, displaying what it means to hold the position of Chief Warrant Officer. In the past year, CW4 Wilson has shown countless acts of leadership, mentorship, and has become a true role model for every Soldier.

CW4 Wilson enlisted in the Ohio Army National Guard May 28, 1980 serving as a tank mechanic in the Headquarters and Headquarters Troop of the 107th Armored Calvary Regiment. His civilian job took him to Sonora, Texas where he served honorably with the 49th Armored Division of Texas Army National Guard as a tank mechanic. Upon his return from Texas in 1983 he returned to HHT 107th ACR and in 1984 promoted to Sergeant. In August 1986, he became a fulltime technician for then Organizational Shop #9. In 1988, he served as Motor Sergeant and in 1989 gained the additional duty as Platoon Sergeant. In 1993, the 107th ACR disbanded and with the action came the closing of the Green Road facility to include the Organizational Maintenance Shop.

In September 1993, militarily he was transferred to Detachment 1 of the 214th Maintenance Company in Medina Ohio becoming an Automotive Inspector. His fulltime position was relocated to OMS #8 in Brookpark, Ohio and eventually to Boston Mills, Ohio.

The military move put him in an over grade position for a year and he was laterally moved to the unit headquarters located in Willoughby, OH as the motor sergeant responsible for all maintenance operations which included Detachment 1 214th in located Medina Ohio, Detachment 2 214th located in Ashtabula Ohio and the company headquarters. The Army was going through a reorganization period in which the 214th Maintenance Company became expendable and was transformed into the 372nd Maintenance Company with a Detachment 1 in Medina Ohio, Detachment 2 in Ashtabula Ohio and a new Detachment located in Camp Perry Ohio.

In July 1995, during Annual Training at Camp Grayling, MI. Recognizing his impending retirement then First Sergeant RC Davis selected CW4 Wilson to take over the unit as acting First Sergeant in which he served for 21 months. On April 1, 1997, CW4 Wilson was officially awarded the First Sergeant's position.

In 1995, discussions had begun to reopen the Armory at Green Road and CW4 Wilson was asked to participate on a feasibility study board with then COL Deborah Ashenhurst to look at what it would take to make it a reality. During this time 1SG Wilson and CPT Randall Rogers proposed the idea of consolidating Willoughby and Medina at Green Road leaving a Detachment at Camp Perry. Detachment 2 located in Ashtabula OH was then reassigned to the 237th FSB Headquartered at Camp Ravenna, n Newton Falls, OH. After the consolidation, the 372nd and 211th maintenance companies were tasked with a 3-week training rotation at the National Training Center at FT Irwin CA. CW4 worked two weekends per month traveling from Cleveland, OH to Newark, OH ensuring each unit had equal attention and was fully prepared to execute the mission which turned out to be a huge success.

In January 1999, CW4 Wilson left the 372nd and took the Senior Maintenance Supervisor position at Service Battery 134th Field Artillery in Medina, OH.

In September 2000, CW4 Wilson was selected to become the fulltime Shop Supervisor for OMS #26 located in Austintown OH where he served in that capacity for 5 years.

In November 2000, because of his fulltime position change, he left the 134th FA to join the 237th Forward Support Battalion in Newton Falls, OH as the Maintenance Control Sergeant. While serving in this position CW4 Wilson thought he could better serve the Army as a Warrant Officer. CW4 Wilson attended The Warrant Officer Career Center located at FT. Rucker Alabama and upon completion of Warrant Officer Candidate school in February 2002, he became the first candidate to be granted a waiver due to his previous enlisted rank of E-8 and being qualified in 5 different maintenance military occupational specialties, earning him the honor of being promoted from W01 to CW2 immediately after his graduation. Upon his return to the 237th FSB he was transferred to Detachment 2 of the 237th FSB in Ashtabula OH where he was assigned as the Detachment Commander and Maintenance Control Officer.

In June 2004, duty called and CW4 Wilson was transferred to Headquarters 37th Armored Brigade in Columbus, OH and mobilized for Operation Joint Guard, Taskforce KFOR 6A in Kosovo, where he served as the G4 Material Readiness Officer overseeing all property, maintenance and transportation operations for Camp Bondsteel and Camp Montief, because of his straight forwardness, due diligence and tenacity, he was asked to conduct the surveillance on contractors and DOD civilians in theater, in which he quickly became affectionately known by civilians and contractors as "That Chief from Ohio".

Upon his return in March 2005, CW4 Wilson saw an opportunity to return to Cleveland, as the shop supervisor for Field Maintenance Shop #3. CW4 Wilson made the case to be command directed back to the facility in which his fulltime career had started. This move of course created a situation where he had to change units sending him back to the 372nd Maintenance Company where he was welcomed with open arms.

In September 2006, the 372nd Disbanded and subsequently became Alpha Company 237th BSB. The lineage, colors and honors of the 372nd went to the 237th Brigade Support Battalion and CW4 Wilson was assigned to the Senor Maintenance WO position in HHC 237th BSB. While serving in this capacity he worked as the Maintenance

Control Officer for Bravo Co. 237th and as the Brigade Maintenance Officer for the 37th IBCT (Infantry Brigade Combat Team).

In July of 2007, CW4 Wilson was called up again to serve our country and in March 2008 was mobilized to Kuwait as the Executive Officer of B Co. 237th BSB. His primary mission was to oversee the maintenance operations in Camp Virginia and Camp Buehring ensuring convoy security and Area Reaction and Quick Reaction Force (ARF/QRF) vehicles were 100% ready to move shoot and communicate. During this deployment, his commander suffered and injury and was sent back to the US for rehabilitation and the Battalion Command selected CW4 Wilson to serve as company commander. For the duration of the mission his focus was the Battle Desk Operations Center (BDOC) and the left seat right seat training with the replacement unit.

In Oct 2009, CW4 Wilson was assigned to the newly stood up 212th Support Maintenance Company in Medina OH becoming one of the original 12 members tasked with growing the company.

In February of 2014, CW4 Wilson developed and implemented an excel spreadsheet to monitor and assess the Commander's Drivers Training and License Program that was an incredible asset to not only the Commander, but also to the seven young Lieutenants he had taken under his wing to mentor for a year. This document was well received by the State COMET Team and adopted as the standard for the State of Ohio. CW4 Wilson's vast experience and knowledge in maintenance, military history, leadership, values, and everyday life decisions has helped shape and mold his 3rd generation of Lieutenants adding to the already long list, into effective Officers in the United States Army.

CW4 Wilson demonstrated outstanding professional skill, knowledge, and leadership in preparing and deploying 372nd equipment in 2005 for Hurricane Katrina and as of late, Operation Guardian Neptune in August 2014. With less than 12 hours' notice, CW4 Wilson worked hard with small unit teams from the 212th SMC to inspect and validate equipment readiness for Alpha Co. 237th BSB and get them ready to deploy to Toledo during that cities water crisis.

CW4 Wilson's actions and dedication to this country was finally recognized when he was awarded the Order of Samuel Sharpe Award on January 22, 2015. The purpose of the Ordnance Order of Samuel Sharpe is to recognize those individuals who have served the United States Army Ordnance Corps with demonstrated integrity, moral character and professional competence over a sustained period of time. And whose selfless contributions to the Corps stand out in the eyes of their seniors, peers and subordinates alike. CW4 Wilson's actions are in keeping with the finest traditions of military service and reflect distinct credit upon himself, this command, and the United States Army.

In April 2015, CW4 Wilson was transferred to the Senior Ordnance Ground Maintenance Officer position at the ARNG ELEM JFHQ (-) of the OHARNG located in Columbus, OH, where he currently serves as a Command Maintenance evaluator, Mobilization and Demobilization Tiger team OIC and Logistic team member and part of a training Cadre for the State Maintenance Officer Course.

As a fulltime technician, CW4 Wilson has served as a board member for the National Guard Professional Education Center located at Camp Robinson AK, assisting with the design and evaluation of training for State Maintenance Managers and Field Maintenance Shop Supervisors. Commanders at all levels seek him for guidance and recommendations knowing they well get his honest opinion and spot on assessment in multiple areas. He has served as shop supervisor for FMS 3 formerly (OMS 9) Cleveland, and FMS 5 (formerly OMS 26) Austintown; Temporary supervisor at FMS 4 (formerly OMS 2) Stow, and Temporary supervisor of the Unit Training Equipment Site (UTES) Newton Falls; and as an EEO counselor for the State Equal Opportunity Office in Columbus, OH.

Mr. Wilson's awards include: 2-MSM, 4-ARCOM, 4-AR ACHV, OHAWM, OHFSR, OHBC, OHCOM. He received the Order of Samuel Sharpe Award on 22 January 2015. CW4 Wilson retired on 31 December 2017.

Articles By / About African American Warrant Officers

Eagle Rising Society inducts retired CW5 into ranks
By Nathan Pfau, Army Flier Staff Writer June 29, 2017

Retired Air Force Lt. Col. Dana Atkins, Military Officers Association of America president and chief executive officer, and Col. Garry L. Thompson (right), U.S. Army Warrant Officer Career College commandant, induct retired CW5 Rufus N. Montgomery Sr. into the Order of the Eagle Rising Society during a ceremony at the U.S. Army Aviation Museum June 26. (Photo Credit: Nathan Pfau)

FORT RUCKER, Ala. -- After almost four decades of service to the nation, one veteran joined the ranks of some the Army's most storied Aviators with his induction into one of Aviation's most prestigious societies.

Retired CW5 Rufus N. Montgomery Sr. was inducted into the Order of the Eagle Rising Society becoming the 20th member during a ceremony at the U.S. Army Aviation Museum June 26.

"This morning we are privileged to recognize [Montgomery] as the newest member of the Eagle Rising Society," said Col. Garry L. Thompson, U.S. Army Warrant Officer Career College commandant, during the ceremony. "Today, we add Mr. Montgomery's 37 years of dedicated service, not to mention his continued loyalty and contribution to the warrant officer cohort and the surrounding community.

It's now your time to take your rightful place as only one of 20 Americans to have received the Order of the Eagle Rising," he said. "In you we find a sterling example to be emulated, and a reminder of the selfless service that can live within us all."

Montgomery said he was humbled to be inducted into the society, and only ever wished to serve his country and create an environment for others to succeed.

"Today, I have an honor given to only a few select Soldiers -- induction into the Order of the Eagle Rising Society. I accept this honor with gratitude, humility and much respect," he said. "I chose not to do what the Army wanted me to do or go where the road led me. Instead, I did what the Army wanted me to do, but went a little bit further to do more.

"[I chose] to be loyal to my superiors and my subordinates," he continued. "[I chose] to go beyond the road and do more, and create a new road that my fellow Soldiers and civilians could follow and be successful. I'm a very happy man today. Thank you all very much."

Montgomery enlisted into the Army in 1965 during a time when it wasn't popular to be a Soldier, but nevertheless took his place as a combat infantryman (paratrooper) and later as a cook with C Company, 1st Battalion, 503rd Airborne Infantry, 173rd Airborne Brigade in Bien Hoa, Vietnam, during his first tour of duty.

"I had an opportunity to briefly see what was in Rufus' background, and I think the part that stood out the most was the fact that he entered the Army in 1965," said retired Air Force Lt. Col. Dana Atkins, Military Officers Association of America president and chief executive officer, and guest speaker for the event. "This was on the cusp of the Vietnam War. It was when (many in) our nation hated the military. When our service members came back and literally had apples, oranges, rotten grapes, tomatoes, eggs, whatever, were thrown [at them], but yet he elected to give service to his nation, even under that environment.

"He elected to stay 37 more years to serve his nation in a way that no others have done before him," he continued. "Rufus, I can't tell you how much I appreciate this opportunity to now know you personally -- know what you've done and know what you've contributed to the Army through leadership."

From NKAA, Notable Kentucky African Americans Database (main entry)
Payne White, Brenda Phillips

Brenda Phillips Payne White served in Operation Desert Storm and Operation Enduring Freedom. Known then as Brenda Phillips, she was the first African American female Warrant Officer with the Kentucky Army National Guard. She completed the Officers Candidate School (OCS) in 2004, and was the only female that started and graduated with the Traditional Officer Candidate School class. There were two other females in the Accelerated Class who also graduated with the Traditional Class. Brenda Phillips took her Commission on September 1, 2005. Her highest rank was CW2 (Chief Warrant Officer II). In 2011, Brenda P. Paynewhite was a veteran and a volunteer with a nonprofit organization in Lexington, KY, called Veterans Outreach. The charitable organization provided assistance to veterans by covering some of the social services gaps. From 2008-2009, Brenda P. Paynewhite was a fundraiser, she was the volunteer coordinator and assistant program director through VISTA (Volunteers In Service To America) for the King Center in Frankfort, KY. Brenda P. Paynewhite was born in Georgia and resides in Frankfort, KY, where she is a notary signing agent for Kentucky. The name of her business is Bluegrass Signing Agent and Consulting LLC. The Chamber of Commerce in Frankfort did the ribbon cutting when the business opened in 2009 at 624 Shelby Street. The business is listed in

OpenCorporates: The Open Database of the Corporate World. Brenda P. Paynewhite is also a Kentucky Colonel, and she is the author of the 2012 published poem "Please Don't Utter a Word." For more information see "WO1 Brenda J. Phillips KYARNG" in *GX [Guard Experience]*, v.2, issue 6, p.36 [online]; M. Davis, "Agency closes gaps in veteran's social services – Success leads to second office in Kentucky," *Lexington Herald-Leader*, 07/10/2011, city/region section, p.B1 [online version]; and B. J. S. Paynewhite, "Please Don't Utter a Word," *Journal of Military Experience*, v.2, issue 2, Article 51 [online].

"Paynewhite, Brenda Phillips," *Notable Kentucky African Americans Database*, accessed November 10, 2017, https://nkaa.uky.edu/nkaa/items/show/3162.

Black History Month profile: Chief Warrant Officer Donald Smith

Army Chief Warrant Officer Donald Smith, a food safety officer for the Defense Health Agency, serves as a role-model for younger service members. 2/9/2016 By: Military System Communications Office

Army Chief Warrant Officer Donald Smith, a food safety officer for the Defense Health Agency, began his military career after graduating from Shamrock High School in Decatur, Georgia, in 1989. A native of Dothan, Alabama, Smith has been a symbol of professionalism and excellence, and serves as a role-model for younger service members.

From day one of his enlistment, Smith 'hit the ground running,' taking part in Operation Just Cause in Panama, earning him his first combat patch. His work ethic earned him Soldier of the Year honors twice as well as Non-Commissioned Officer of the Year. Smith quickly ascended to the rank of Staff Sgt. and was urged to apply for Warrant Officer School by his superiors.

When he was promoted to the rank of Chief Warrant officer one, Smith became the first warrant officer in the Army to take over a district command, overseeing food safety for service members in Latin America and the Caribbean.

Smith says his late mother – Barbara Smith – served as his role-model, and instilled in him a sense of pride and self-determination. "My mother was a very strong woman," he said. "Even though we were less fortunate growing up, she always got on me and my brothers about having good manners, speaking properly and having a sense of pride about ourselves. She also stressed the importance of having sense of self-worth, and never feeling or thinking we were less than anyone else because we were poor."

He mentioned how his mother overcame many struggles to get an education, despite the burden of being a single parent. "Seeing her work multiple jobs just to make sure we would have basic necessities, and pushing forward to get her GED and eventually a nursing degree really showed me the value of getting an education," Smith said. "Once she earned her nursing degree, she was able to get a better job, and we were able to move from Alabama to the suburbs of Atlanta."

With regard to prominent African-Americans, Smith says abolitionist Frederick Douglass had the most impact on him. "To me, Frederick Douglass embodied many of the characteristics that I saw in my mother," he said. "He taught himself how to read and write, and it was after he became educated that he became more aware of the social injustices that he had dealt with throughout his life. And in gaining a better education, it was his goal to help other slaves get an education as well."

Smith also credits Army Col. Sherry Graham, senior veterinarian for the Army Public Health Command-Atlantic Region, for serving as a mentor, and helping shape the direction of his military career. "Col. Graham was the one who re-affirmed in me as a leader that one of our greatest assets is the people we work with, as well as the people work for," he said. "She also helped me understand the human side of people we work with, and that everyone we encounter presents an opportunity to learn, grow and become a better person."

With the Army Veterinary Corps celebrating its 100th anniversary, Smith said he is proud of the contributions that warrant officers have made to food safety. "It is really an honor to know that the hard work we have done, and continue to do, has influence in other sectors," he said. "The Food and Drug Administration is now looking to incorporate some of the measures we use to ensure food safety in their own protocols."

Lastly, Smith says he is proud of all he has accomplished, and takes great pride in being able to make tangible contributions as a service member. "This is a great nation we live in, and I'm proud to have been fortunate to do so since I was 17 years old," he said. "To have traveled to more than 30 countries, and be able to serve in various capacities, is an honor that I will continue to cherish."

ARMY✛FLIER

WOCC renames awards in veterans' honor

By Nathan Pfau, Army Flier Staff Writer June 25, 2015

Retired CW3 Doris Allen presents WO1 Emanuel Medinasoto with the CW3 (R) Doris Allen Distinguished Honor Graduate Award during a U.S. Army Warrant Officer Career College graduation ceremony June 17 at the U.S. Army Aviation Museum as Col. Garry L. Thompson, WOCC commandant, looks on.

The past and present of the warrant officer cohort merged as two U.S. Army Warrant Officer Candidate School awards were renamed in honor of two storied veterans and presented to two of the Army's newest warrant officers June 17.

The school renamed its Distinguished Honor Graduate Award and Leadership Award to the CW3 (R) Doris Allen Distinguished Honor Graduate Award and the CW4 (R) William L. Ruf Award, respectively, and presented the awards for the first time under their new monikers during a graduation ceremony at the U.S. Army Aviation Museum.

"I think it is great that we are able to honor two heroes of our Army and the warrant officer cohort," said Col. Garry L. Thompson, U.S. Army Warrant Officer Career College commandant. "We've been presenting the awards to candidates for over 20 years, so naming the awards was long overdue."

It was a process, he added, that took nearly a year after submitting and coordinating nomination packets.

The first recipients of the renamed awards were WO1 Emanuel Medinasoto, recipient of the CW3 (R) Doris Allen DHG Award, and WO1 Matthew Cook, recipient of the CW4 (R) William L. Ruf Award.

Allen, who is a Vietnam-era veteran and served 30 years in the Army, was available to present the award during the ceremony, and she said she was honored to do so.

"I was invited to attend and I consider it quite an honor for them to invite me and for me to be there," she said. "I think it's historic. To lend authenticity is so important, and I want to be able to be the one that can come and do that here.

"It's also just a proud moment," she continued. "If I had no humility, I'd be jumping on the ceiling. After all that I've been through, it's just an honor – period."

Allen enlisted into the Women's Army Corp in 1950 and entered the Army as an entertainment specialist at the Adjutant General School in 1951 at Fort Lee, Virginia. She had a storied career, assigned as a radio broadcast specialist at Camp Stoneman, California, and served five years as an information specialist for the headquarters at Fort Monmouth, New Jersey, before completing French language training in 1963 and becoming the first military female trained in a prisoner of war interrogation course at the U.S. Army Intelligence School at Fort Holabird, Maryland.

As a specialist seven, Allen reported to Vietnam as the senior intelligence analyst for Army Operations Center, Headquarters, U.S. Army at Long Binh, Vietnam. She began her second tour in Vietnam and by spring of 1970 she was appointed as a warrant officer – one of only nine female warrant officers in military intelligence and one of only 23 in the Army.

She returned to the U.S. in September of 1970 after completing her third tour in Vietnam, and she served as an instructor for prisoner of war interrogations. She would be promoted to chief warrant officer three before retiring from the Army in 1980.

The late Ruf, whose wife, Kim, was available to present the award, is well known in the Aviation world and even has a street named after him on Fort Rucker.

He was a pioneer in Aviation, having graduated from the first rotary-wing flight class at Fort Rucker in 1955. He eventually went on to serve as a helicopter pilot for two presidents: Dwight D. Eisenhower and John F. Kennedy.

Ruf also served as an infantryman in World War II, as well as a pilot in the Korean War, and volunteered as an Aviator in the Vietnam War. During his 26-year Army career, he accumulated more than 16,000 total flight hours, 1,200 of which were in combat, before retiring in 1967. He continued to serve as a flight instructor after his Army service.

Regardless of the storied lives of the two warrant officers the awards are named after, Allen said the takeaway for young Soldiers should be that nothing in the Army is a single effort, but it is the efforts of many that make the Army great.

"When you're in the military, if you don't do it together then it won't get done," said Allen. "We're born, we live and we die. The best we can do is to live the best we can through it all."

Signal Warrant Officer signs off the net one last time

Photo By Sgt. Jennifer Amo | Brig. Gen. George M. Degnon, acting Adjutant
General, District of Columbia National

WASHINGTON, DC, UNITED STATES
05.07.2017
Story by Maj. Byron Coward

WASHINGTON, D.C. (May 7, 2017) – The D.C. National Guard held a retirement ceremony to honor its former Command Chief Warrant Officer at the D.C. National Guard Armory today.

Chief Warrant Officer 5 Janice L. Fontanez, an Athens, Georgia native, retired from the D.C. Army National Guard after exactly 41 years, 9 months and 16 days of military service. Her last assignment was as the Fourth Command Chief Warrant Officer of the D.C. National Guard. Prior to her retirement ceremony, she relinquished responsibility of the Command Chief Warrant Officer position to Chief Warrant Officer 5 Michael R. Jewett.

Fontanez was one of the few remaining, active, female service members who enlisted in the Army Women's Corps. She also held the distinction of being one of the six longest-serving women in the army and was the only female, U.S. Army Signal Corps, Chief Warrant Officer 5 in the National Guard.

In 1975, Fontanez began her military career enlisting in the Army Reserves to help pay for school. In 1976, she attended the Women's Army Corps' Basic Combat Training, Ft. Jackson, South Carolina.

"When we all arrived at the WOC reception center, we were excited and really did not know what to expect," Fontanez said. "They divided us up, and I was one of the recruits assigned to go to Basic Training in Ft. Jackson. When we arrived, we met our drill instructor and everything changed."

Fontanez recalled an instance where the drill instructor brought in a record and played the Sonny and Cher song "I've got you, Babe." When the instructor stopped the record player, during the song, all the recruits continued the song in chorus.

"That's when I knew I was a part of something special," Fontanez said. "The camaraderie in our unit was amazing and I knew then that we are going to make it."

After basic training, she attended Advanced Individual Training to become a 74D, Computer Systems Operator, at Ft. Ben Harrison, Indiana

In 1978, Fontanez moved to Washington, D.C. to take a civilian job with the FBI and joined the D.C. National Guard later that year. She eventually became a Military Technician with the U.S. Property and Fiscal Office, or USPFO, working as a keypunch operator. While at the USPFO she progressed from a keypunch operator to computer operator, and finally to a programmer/systems analysts while reaching the rank of Sgt. 1st Class.

In 1988 she was selected to be a Signal Warrant Officer and attended the National Guard's Warrant Officer Candidate School at Ft. McCoy, Wisconsin. She was the first female, and first non-aviation candidate, from the DCNG to attend and complete the school. This was immediately followed by the Signal Warrant Officer Basic Course at Ft. Gordon, Georgia where she received her appointment as a Warrant Officer 1 in 1989.

Fontanez's career encompasses the incorporation of the D.C. National Guard into the information age. She was responsible for the analog to digital conversion of the D.C. Armory phone system and introduced the DCNG to the World Wide Web and e-mail.

In 2003 she was selected for a tour at National Guard Bureau to be a webmaster for Guard Knowledge Online portal and assisted in it full integration into the National Guard. During the aftermath of Hurricane

Katrina, she assisted the Louisiana and Mississippi National Guards in reconstructing their web-based systems.

In 2011, she was selected to be the Army National Guard, Senior Signal Warrant Officer Advisor to the Deputy Assistant Commandant of the 442nd Signal Battalion, Cyber Leader College at the U.S. Army's Cyber Center of Excellence at Fort Gordon, Georgia. Additionally, she was Warrant Officer Intermediate Level Education Course manager and implemented a pipeline for the course to support both Army National Guard and Reserve Warrant Officers.

In 2013, she returned to the National Guard Bureau as the Senior Signal Warrant Officer Advisor to the communications directorate. While there she managed all Signal Warrant Officers on Title 10 orders and supported all National Guard Signal Warrant Officers.

Fontanez returned to the D.C. National Guard, in 2015 to be the Command Chief Warrant Officer. In a span of one year, she led a change that elevated metrics specific to warrant officer qualification, readiness, promotions, accessions and professional military education.

"It is amazing to see, in our time, the increasing role of women, and their responsibilities, in our armed forces," said Brig. Gen. William J. Walker, acting Commanding General, D.C. National Guard. "This progress has been made possible by women like Chief Fontanez who get after it and do great things."

During the retirement ceremony, Fontanez was awarded the Legion of Merit and the D.C. National Guard Distinguished Service Medal.

**Only African American female to serve as rigger
warrant officer retires**
By Sgt. Daniel Cole, U.S. Army Europe Public Affairs December 18, 2014

WIESBADEN, Germany -- The day a Soldier retirees from their military service is one filled with many emotions, both positive and negative, this can be especially true when the Soldier's story is unique.

Chief Warrant Officer 4 Petrice McKey-Reese is one of those unique Soldiers. Her retirement ceremony, held here Dec. 17, marked the final page in her 30-year career as a parachute rigger, 21 of those years as a warrant officer, and the only African American female to ever be designated a rigger warrant.

Born in New Orleans, La., McKey-Reese grew up around rich culture, which she only realized after leaving for the military. The well-known food, people and music associated with the southern city are regularly on her mind as she longs for a taste of home

Months after her 18th birthday she decided that family came first and that she wanted her two-year-old son to have a better way of life; to do that a sacrifice needed to be made to ensure her son had a positive future. April 24, 1984 was the day she began building upon that dream and left the "Crescent City" for basic training at Fort McClellan, Alabama.

Fast forward nine years in the future, Staff Sgt. McKey-Reese drew the attention of her senior leaders as a stand-out Soldier who could hold her own in a predominantly male field.

"Retired Chief Warrant Officer 4 Robert Ford, retired Col. Gloria Blake and retired Sgt. 1st Class Marshall Ford saw something in me as a young Soldier and they thought I would make a good warrant officer," McKey-Reese said. "I also wanted to change some things in our field."

At the time, her field only had one female warrant officer, Chief Warrant Officer 4 Debra Lee, now retired, and was someone the hopeful noncommissioned officer admired.

Hoping to make the change a reality, McKey-Reese headed to Fort Rucker in southern Alabama during the winter of 1993 to pursue her transition to warrant officer.

Her Airdrop Systems Technician training lasted approximately 20 weeks and during those weeks she learned how to support commanders with airborne operations guidance, oversee airdrop and rigger operations, and how to find malfunctions in equipment that potentially saves lives on the drop zone.

McKey-Reese says her most memorable time as a warrant officer was her first mission as a newly pinned warrant about 20 years ago in Haiti. She explained that the mission was an eye opener for her and that the blinders came off; her way of looking at situations through the eyes of an NCO quickly changed. She was developing the perspective of a warrant officer who was seeing a bigger picture.

Moving ahead in time to her retirement ceremony, McKey-Reese was honored by Col. Thomas Stackpole, USAREUR's chief of logistics operations and key speaker at the ceremony, who spoke strongly about her great accomplishments.

"I am proud to have served with Chief McKey-Reese and she will certainly be missed, especially that infection positive attitude she has," Stackpole said.

As McKey-Reese approached the podium to give her speech; as the retiring warrant officer looked around the room, tears came to her eyes which seemed to be filled a bit by sadness and a bit by joy but mostly with the passion that came from the love of her job and the love she has for being a Soldier.

"This moment is bittersweet, as with all major decisions in life, but I am ready to move on to the next chapter," the retiring Soldier said. "I will miss the bonds that have been built over the last 30 years, for I have worked with some of the most outstanding Soldiers, NCOs, officers and warrant officers."

These were part of the final words by McKay-Reese during the ceremony held for a truly unique Soldier. After she was congratulated by all in attendance, some even came back to thank her again for her incredible career and the legacy she will be leaving behind as the first African American female to hold her military occupation.

"Follow your dream," she said with a silvery tone after the ceremony. "Whatever your dream is, follow your dream and keep pushing forward."

Oklahoma Army National Guard promotion makes history
By 1st Lt. Leanna Litsch For The Oklahoman| September 6, 2016

The Oklahoma Army National Guard made history last month with the promotion of the first African-American to achieve the rank of chief warrant officer 5, the highest warrant officer rank.

Tampa, Fla., native Melvin Murphy, now a resident of Moore, celebrated his achievement among a room full of family, friends and colleagues and spoke about being the first of his race within the Oklahoma Army National Guard to reach chief warrant officer 5.

That's a position I do not take lightly," Murphy said. "I want to be that inspiration to the subordinates and actually be that individual that they can look at me and say, 'If CW5 Murphy can do it, I can do it as well.'"

Wearing his new rank for the first time, Murphy spoke at times with a shaky voice in an attempt to hold back his tears as he thanked those who helped him. He mentioned God, his family and retired Chief Warrant Officer 4 David C. Credell, who mentored and encouraged him to become a warrant officer.

According to the state command chief warrant officer for Oklahoma, Chief Warrant Officer 5 Christopher Rau, only one in 100 warrant officer candidate graduates attain the rank of chief warrant officer 5.

"One must be properly prepared through military and civilian education, show great potential to serve with increased responsibility, but then stars must align and luck and timing does come into play," Rau said. Warrant officers are considered master-level technical experts, combat leaders, trainers and advisers. In the Army, they often are pilots of rotary or fixed-wing aircraft.

In Murphy's case, he is the subject matter expert for all things logistics and supply. Specifically, he is the full-time consolidated property book officer in Joint Force Headquarters' logistics section.

"Chief Murphy is one of the most professional solders I have met," said Lt. Col. Steven Stanford, supervisory management specialist. "His willingness to assist, train and mentor soldiers has greatly increased the readiness throughout all levels of the organization.

Murphy's military journey began when he enlisted for active duty in the Army in 1986. Shortly after basic and supply training, Murphy was stationed at Fort Bliss, Texas, before serving as a supply clerk in South Korea for a year. When he returned from Korea, he was stationed at Fort Sill, where he would later join the Guard.

Murphy stayed enlisted for 10 years until commissioning as a warrant officer in 1996. He served in the state Guard's 45th Infantry Brigade Combat Team, and deployed to Afghanistan in support of Operation Enduring Freedom.

1st Lt. Leanna Litsch is with the Oklahoma National Guard.

Army Reserve Soldier named president of local Warrant Officers Association Chapter
By Staff Sgt. David Clemenko April 8, 2016

Caption – (Photo Credit: U.S. Army)

JOINT BASE MCGUIRE-DIX-LAKEHURST, NJ -- The Doughboy Chapter of the U.S. Army Warrant Officers Association recently installed their new president at chapter headquarters here.

"The association is a lifeline for us to give back to the community," said CW4 Keith R. Prather, senior legal administrator for the Army Reserve's 99th Regional Support Command. "It's not just fellowship, it's our volunteer arm to give back to the community through various outreach programs."

Prather joined the USAWOA in 1997 when he graduated from Warrant Officer Candidate School. The USAWOA is the only military service organization maintained by and for Warrant Officers. Their chapters work in the community across the country and give warrant officers of all branches a place to meet and give back to the community.

"I've been a member of the Fort Knox chapter as well as the Atlanta chapter, said Prather. "The Atlanta Chapter was dormant and I activated it and became the president."

The Doughboy Chapter has several community outreach programs they are currently working on, to include scholarships awarded to two local Pemberton High School students every year, food drives, a suit drive for those who are unemployed and need a suit for job interviews, and care packages sent to deployed Army Reserve Soldiers serving in Afghanistan.

"The members of this chapter have been my family while I serve away from my home as a geographical bachelor," said Prather. "They have made the quality of this tour really nice and exciting for me."

Prather joined the Army in August 1978. After successfully completing his first active-duty tour, Prather joined the Army Reserve, which gave him the flexibility to continue to serve and go to college.

Prather became a drill sergeant and stayed in this capacity for the next six years, followed by several years training new Soldiers to the Public Affairs field as a journalist and broadcaster. As a master sergeant in Public Affairs, he had the opportunity to apply for the Warrant Officer Program.

"I was eligible for sergeant major, but I didn't know what the future would hold or if there were any openings," said Prather. "I put my warrant-officer packet in, and a few months later I was accepted."

While Prather was officially a warrant officer in the human-resources field, he continued as an appointed public affairs officer in his unit. Prather served in public affairs, including a tour in Iraq, until he became a CW3 and moved into the staff judge advocate field.

Prather will leave New Jersey this summer to take on his next role as the senior warrant officer/deputy command chief warrant officer for the U.S. Army Reserve Legal Command in Gaithersburg, Maryland.

For any retired, prior-service or currently serving warrant officers interested in joining the Doughboy Chapter of the USAWOA, contact CW4 Keith R. Prather at keith.r.prather.mil@mail.mil or CW3 Misty Whetung at misty.l.whetung.mil@mail.mil or visit the chapter's website at http://woaonline.org/doughboy/.

The chapter meets the third Thursday of every month at Pudgy's Sports Bar and Grill here. There is an occasional Saturday meeting for members who are not local but want to be involved. If you are in another state and looking for the closest chapter, go to the USAWOA website at www.usawoa.org

TRADOC NEWS CENTER
WELCOME TO U.S. ARMY TRAINING AND DOCTRINE COMMAND'S
OFFICIAL NEWS BLOG

21 October 2016

**Meet Your Army: Warrant officer heads up
Army's maritime training**

October 21, 2016. by Keith Desbois, Combined Arms Support Command. Posted in Acquiring the Army, Featured, Frontpage, Meet your Army

JOINT BASE LANGLEY-EUSTIS, Va. — Chief Warrant Officer 5 Jermain C. Williamson is a marine deck officer in the Army.

He serves as the chief of the Maritime Training Division, Maritime Intermodal Training Department at the Army Transportation School, Joint Base Langley-Eustis, Virginia.

Williamson grew up in Portsmouth, Virginia, and is the son of a Navy veteran. He graduated from I.C. Norcom High School and attended Old Dominion University in Norfolk for almost two years before deciding to join the Army.

The 25-year career Soldier said he has been blessed with a number of great assignments during his time in the Army.

"My career started in 1991 as Pvt. Williamson at Fort Story, Virginia, with the 309th Transportation Company. I joined the warrant officer corps in 1999, and I have had a number of challenging assignments as a warrant officer since then," he said.

Williamson has been deployed in many leadership positions, including commanding the 411th Transportation Detachment in Kuwait and serving as operations officer for the 7th Transportation Brigade Expeditionary Staff in Iraq. He was the first African American in his job field to be promoted to chief warrant officer 5, the highest warrant rank.

Aside from serving as an inspiration for his Soldiers, Williamson's career choice made an impression on his two daughters, who today are both serving in the Army.

"A couple of my fondest memories were when my youngest daughter, a second lieutenant, administered the oath of office when I was promoted to chief warrant officer 5 and when I had the honor of administering the oath of enlistment to my oldest daughter when she joined the Army Reserve," he said.

Q&A

Q: What is your hometown?
A: Portsmouth, Virginia.
Q: What is your favorite thing about your hometown?
A: It is a historic military city with a great athletic heritage.
Q: What is the least favorite thing about your hometown?
A: Relatively small city with big-city crime.
Q: As a kid, what did you want to be when you grew up?
A: My initial goal was to be a lawyer when I grew up.
Q: What were your childhood hobbies?
A: Sports. I participated in football, baseball and basketball.
Q: What are your current hobbies?
A: Weight training.
Q: What motivated you to join the Army?
A: To serve my country and provide a better life for my family.

Q: What's your favorite line from your favorite movie?

A: "The force is strong with this one … " from the original Star Wars movie.

Q: What do you consider as your strongest personal strength?

A: My Christian faith.

Q: What challenges have you faced in the military?

A: The normal Soldier challenges of deployments, peer pressure and remembering you are a Soldier 24/7.

Q: What do you consider your most significant achievements in the Army?

A: Being assigned as the first Transportation Corps warrant officer to teach at the Warrant Officer Career College at Fort Rucker, Alabama, and my promotion to chief warrant officer 5.

Q: What are the keys to leadership?

A: Having excellent interpersonal skills.

Q: What do you consider to be the most important Army value?

A: I believe they are all interconnected and equally important.

Pictured above: Chief Warrant Officer 5 Jermain C. Williamson receives the Oath of Office by his youngest daughter, 2nd Lt. Jazmyne Williamson, during his promotion ceremony. (Photo Credit: Joint Base LangleyEustis).

Chief warrant officer conquers adversity, pushes limits
By Adriane Foss USASAC Public Affairs
Apr 22, 2015

Making history in the military was not the plan.

Before he became the first African-American to be promoted to the rank of chief warrant officer 5 in the Army's Transportation Corps, a young Richard Turner wasn't sure what to do with himself.

Growing up in Chicago's gang-riddled inner city during the 1980s made life uncertain.

"Being jumped or held up at knife point, or having your bike stolen, was common in my neighborhood," he said. "I had friends who were killed due to gang activities throughout my high school, so you learn to adapt to your environment. You use your street smarts to stay out of danger."

To stay off the streets and out of trouble, Turner earned a basketball scholarship at a local junior college and spent his time on the courts and in the classroom. But, he said, trouble eventually found him and prompted him to make one of the best decisions of his life.

While at the bus stop late one afternoon, on his way to a home game in which he was the starting power forward, he was held at gunpoint by area gang members. Gang members cried "shoot him, shoot him" as the attacker held the cocked revolver to Turner's chest. Hands raised and duffel bag slung across his shoulder, Turner said he froze.

"My life flashed before my eyes and everything I remembered doing as a kid ran across my mind," he said.

It was a stroke of luck, or destiny, when another teen – confined to a wheelchair after being shot in a previous gang encounter – happened by and was able to convince his buddies that Turner was a decent guy and they could let him go.

Shaken, but not deterred, Turner made it to the basketball game, "unproductive at first. I couldn't stop my hands from shaking in the first quarter, but I settled down and had a good game."

After that close call, Turner realized a truth that would serve him well throughout his distinguished military career: Adversity is par for the course, and perseverance is the key to success.

"Learning to deal with and overcome hardship, misfortune and difficulty is what makes us who we are, makes us stronger. In my experience, maintaining a positive attitude, which can sometimes be an even greater challenge in the midst of a storm, is what will help you persevere."

After the gang encounter at the bus stop, Turner's uncle convinced him to leave Chicago's gritty streets in search of better opportunities. On Oct. 9, 1990, at age 18, he joined the Navy as a seaman deckhand. But it was a tough sell for Turner's mom and biggest fan.

"When I left for boot camp, she wasn't too happy; her baby was leaving home and becoming a man. It was difficult for her to let go, but she's always been a strong woman, and she is the one who motivates me," Turner said of his 68-year-old mother, a cancer survivor. "To see what she has experienced in life and how she has pushed through, it is my reason for surviving."

The Navy was a good fit for Turner. He transferred from deckhand to engineman and quickly reached the rank of petty officer 2nd class. Eager and impressionable, he came into contact with several chief warrant officers who would influence his life course.

"I ultimately chose the warrant officer path because of two great warrant officers early in my Navy career. The first African-American officer I had ever seen was a warrant officer, CW2 Zebedee Clark," Turner said. "He was a boatswain mate onboard the shipping port ARDM-4 and he was very intelligent and hardworking. I watched him, secretly, and witnessed his ability to create a cohesive working environment just by his presence."

Turner said he picked Clark's brain, hoping to follow in his footsteps.

"I wanted to be like him. He probably doesn't remember me or doesn't know how much he influenced me, but wherever he is, I would like to thank him for being the person he was," Turner said.

And then there was Chief Warrant Officer 2 Wayne Adgie.

"He was my auxiliary officer onboard the USS Cape St. George CG-71. He was very intelligent, extremely rugged and the best engineer I have ever witnessed," Turner said. "If sailors were huddled around, not working and just shooting the breeze, if you caught wind that he was coming, we would all scatter because no one wanted to feel his wrath."

One day, Turner was chatting with shipmates when Adgie appeared. As the young sailors scattered up ladder wells and disappeared into hatches, anything to avoid the stern warrant officer, Turner stood fast.

"I didn't run. I wanted to see what he would say or do. He walked up to me and we had a great conversation about my family, where I am from and what I wanted to do with my life," Turner said. "After that he became a father figure to me, as well as a great mentor and my biggest influence."

With a newfound confidence, borne from observing great leaders in action, Turner knew it was again time to change the course of his life.

With eight successful Navy years under his belt, Turner joined the Army, immediately beginning training at the Warrant Officer Candidate School, Fort Rucker.

"Leaving the Navy as an E-5 enlisted sailor into the Army's Warrant Officer Procurement Program and achieving the rank of CW5 is unprecedented," Turner said of his historic achievement.

And switching from the Navy to the Army meant new customs, standards and jargon. "Just learning to march was pure comedy for my classmates during Warrant Officer Candidate School," he said.

But Turner did learn. And he excelled.

"What makes any person successful is falling down nine times and getting up 10. If you want something bad enough, put your whole being into it and the universe will allow things to happen for you."

After graduating candidate school, Turner's first junior warrant officer assignment was serving as the assistant engineering officer aboard the Army's Large Tug for the 73rd Transportation Company, Fort Eustis, Virginia. Eight months later he became the chief engineer of the Large Tug.

Commanders began to seek him out for his technical expertise. Technical expertise, after all, is what makes a warrant officer unique, Turner explained.

Unlike commissioned officers, warrants are enlisted service members initially appointed by the secretary of the Army and then commissioned by the president of the United States upon promotion to chief warrant officer. They are technically focused, single specialty officers who undergo rigorous education and training to develop subject matter expertise.

"We are the continuity between enlisted Soldiers and officers," Turner said. "A lieutenant or a captain will have a basic understanding about different systems, that warrant knows almost everything about the system. Commanders rely on this expertise and leadership ability to provide guidance in our fields."

According to the Army Human Resources Command, there are about 15,000 warrant officers in the Army, making up around 2.4 percent of the total force, and close to 15 percent of the officer corps. Most warrant officers previously served as enlisted Soldiers.

Never one to shy from challenge, Turner's next assignment was chief engineer for the 97th Transportation Heavy Boat Company, Fort Eustis. He served on several vessels before deploying to Kuwait where he assumed responsibility for several boats in support of Operation Iraqi Freedom.

Turner redeployed and served as supply officer aboard the Logistic Support Vessel at Ford Island, Hawaii, before a second deployment to Kuwait. In Kuwait, he was promoted to chief warrant officer 3 and became the 545th Transportation Company executive officer at Hickam Air Force Base, Hawaii.

He later served as the battalion marine maintenance officer, Fort Eustis; chief engineer for a Department of Defense counter-drug interdiction vessel, Norfolk, Virginia; and maintenance officer for the 558th Transportation Company, Fort Eustis. After a third deployment to Kuwait, he returned to the United States to assume command of the 545th Harbormaster Detachment, eventually fielding the unit's Harbormaster Command and Control Center and receiving honors for commanding the best trained harbormaster detachment in the Army.

He said his time as commander of the Harbormaster Detachment was, by far, his favorite assignment. As an 881A marine engineering officer, the chances were slim that he would command a detachment. There are only two warrant officer specialties that offer detachment commands, and his was not one of them.

"I should not have been afforded that chance, but my leadership had confidence in me; it was a unique opportunity for a warrant officer," he said. "As detachment commander, I got to lead Soldiers, build cohesion and make our unit family friendly. I took care of them, and they took care of me. I can honestly say if it wasn't for them, I wouldn't be a CW5 today. It was their hard work and dedication that ranked me No. 1 warrant officer in my brigade two years in a row."

Turner went on to serve as the 45th Sustainment Brigade's chief of watercraft operations and the unit's senior warrant officer, responsible for the welfare, training, mentoring and job placement of all officers in the brigade at Schofield Barracks, Hawaii.

He is currently assigned to the Security Assistance Training Management Organization at Fort Bragg, North Carolina, serving as the chief of the Joint Planning and Assistance Team in Belize City, Belize.

Turner is responsible for advising, training and supervising maintenance for the Belize Coast Guard, Belize Defense Force and Air Wing on activities required for the planning and execution of counter narcotics operations. He is the principal adviser to the senior defense official and defense attaché on all maintenance, operations, communications and training activities for all Belize military vehicles, vessels, aircraft and weapons systems.

On Feb. 1, while serving in this position, he was promoted to chief warrant officer 5, a relatively new rank reserved for the best of the best. The rank of master warrant officer (chief warrant officer 5) was created Dec. 5, 1991, by the Warrant Officer Management Act Pub. L. 102-190.

Turner said he's proud of his historic promotion and will use the opportunity to make a difference in his career field. He said he wants to make a positive impact in the Warrant Officer Corps and the Army's watercraft community by setting high standards. One way he hopes to accomplish this is by inspiring and mentoring junior Soldiers.

For Chief Warrant Officer 2 Jason Milligan, Turner's mentorship was a career booster.

"He took notice that as a new officer I did not have any guidance from other senior personnel, so he stepped in and began to help me, mainly with my transition from enlisted to officer," said Milligan, who has known Turner for five years.

"His work ethic is second to none. He is the kind of person who will not stop at the first correct answer, but will continue to seek out possibilities and options and package it into understandable information that allows you to make the best decision," Milligan said. "And if he doesn't know the answer, which is not often, he will exhaust every avenue to obtain the correct answer."

Milligan also called Turner a humble leader.

"I feel honored that he sees something special in me and takes the time to give wise counsel. But as honored as I feel, I know that he doesn't just focus on me. He offers insight to all junior officers," he said. "He has the whole team in mind when he makes decisions or speaks. A rising tide raises all ships."

Chief Warrant Officer 2 Arian Fernandez agrees and said Turner's technical expertise and candor are two of his greatest leadership traits.

"CW5 Turner defines what a warrant officer is — a true Army professional. His vast knowledge of watercraft systems has been paramount to the planning and execution of several worldwide missions and commitments," said Fernandez, who met Turner during duty with the 545th Transportation Company in Hawaii. "I respect his views and candid responses when it comes to teaching and mentoring. Whether I am right or wrong in any situation, he will find a way to expand my situational awareness and knowledge.

"What I admire most is his ability to go way out of his comfort zone to complete any given task in the military," Fernandez said. "Watercraft engineer is only a title. What he does above and beyond his scope of responsibilities is what speaks leagues about him."

Turner said he emphasizes overcoming adversity and pushing your limits because it worked for him.

"Know that nothing will come easy. Dealing with hardships and misfortune is what makes you stronger. Take care of people along your journey," Turner said, "and ask the people you took care of to pay it forward."

First AGR mobility officer in the Army Reserve to make Chief Warrant Officer 4
By Sgt. 1st Class Lyndon Miller, 412th TEC Public Affairs
March 10, 2014

"Congratulations on your selection for promotion to CW4. This accomplishment reflects great effort and commitment on your part. You are the first AGR 882A to reach this rank and this milestone is well noted. You are leading the way. Your service to your Nation is gratefully acknowledged. Best to you and all your future endeavors."

So wrote U.S. Army Reserve Chief Warrant Officer 4 Tracy Garder, Assignments Officer for the Quartermaster and Transportation Branches at Fort Know, Ky. to Chief Warrant Officer 3 Destria Gladney, G4 Transportation officer in charge with the 412th Theater Engineer Command in Vicksburg, Miss.

"I am actually the very first one in the Army Reserve AGR program to make CW4 in the 882A Mobility Officer military occupational specialty," Gladney said.

AGR, in short for the Active Guard Reserve program, provides full-time Soldiers for Army Reserve and National Guard units.

Her actual promotion will take place in August 2014.

Gladney first enlisted in the Reserve in 1984 in Fairfield, Calif., as an E3 because she had an associate's degree in psychology.

"I ran into an Army recruiter at an air show and he said he could get me in," Gladney said.

Her first job was as a 71D legal specialist in the 221st Legal Detachment based at the Presidio. She held that MOS until 1994.

"The change came when they restructured the legal command. My position was going away," she said.

A friend suggested Gladney get into the transportation field. After looking into it and seeing exactly what they did, she eventually joined the 483th Terminal Transportation Battalion in Vallejo, Calif., as an 88N transportation management coordinator.

With the 483rd Gladney traveled a lot on temporary duty assignments.

I was gone the majority of the time, Gladney said. We went to Port Hueneme, Calif., Puerto Rico, Beaumont, Texas, and Seattle, Wash., and I loved it. We were at a whole lot of places.

In Puerto Rico, I participated in a Joint Logistics Over the Shore exercise, where we loaded equipment onto boats and sent this equipment out to other ships waiting in the sea.

Her main job at the 483rd was as a cargo documentation officer.

I worked with WPS, World-Wide Port Systems, a database that produced the manifests for the boats. I did convoy clearances. I made sure all the equipment coming in and going out of the ports was accounted for, she said.

Another change in Gladney's military career was about happen.

At a truck rodeo at Fort Hunter-Liggett, Calif., in 1999, a warrant officer recruiter was perched on a hill overlooking Gladney's operation below. The recruiter could see what she was doing. Other folks were noticing her, too.

"I guess a lot of people went and told him that I either had roller skates on or was on a bike, because I was moving containers, staging and moving equipment flawlessly, according to them," Gladney said. "Me? I was not paying attention to that. All I wanted to know was that my equipment was moving in and out without a hitch.

The warrant officer recruiter eventually approached Gladney and talked her into applying. "He said to me, 'Here is the information, fill it out now and get it back to me,'" Gladney said.

The warrant officer MOS of 882A mobility officer was brand new. "'You will be one of the first,'" he said to me, "a transportation warrant.'" Gladney was made an 882A Warrant Officer in 2000, the first milestone for her.

"When I started as a warrant, there was a great need for us," Gladney said. However the need was not met with a whole lot of acceptance. Commanders did not know what we were. We were trailblazers."

Big Army "knew they needed somebody to liaison that piece between what the combatant commanders needed and what the supported commanders could do in moving equipment. So, we were in-between the people getting troops out the door and getting them to ground, port to port," she said.

"We were the subject matter experts."

I was with the 483rd until 2003 when I mobilized for nine months with the 511th Movement Control Team to Kuwait," Gladney said.

"I established a centralized shipping and receiving point at Camp Al Sayliyah. We received containers, FEDEX shipments, anything that was coming in. We would receive it and make sure the commanders all over Southwest Asia got their equipment."

Gladney became a full-timer in 2006 and joined AGR program. She was stationed at Fort Benjamin Harrison with the 310th Expeditionary Sustainment Command.

"I was a mobility warrant officer in support operations, and that was the beginning of support operations with sustainment commands," Gladney said. "It was a new thing coming along then."

While with the 310th, Gladney deployed to Iraq in March 2011. "We actually shut down Iraq," Gladney said, "We closed the doors. I did container management and dealt with over 40,000 containers there."

"We were actually attacked a few times. At that time, it was not scary, but coming back home and reflecting on it, it became scary."

Gladney transferred from the 310th ESC to the 412th Theater Engineer Command in June 2013.

At the 412th TEC level, "I am management purely. I manage all the transportation aspects for the 412th TEC. I make sure the right transportation account codes are available, that funding is available. I make sure that the Soldiers working for me are keeping in line with all the regulations and any changes that occur. I manage bus requests, large equipment movement, and travel."

She works with her counterparts in the downtrace units, the logistics management specialists and others at the Brigades to make all this happen.

."We just had a lot of equipment transported to Camp Shelby for the 760th Engineer Company," Gladney said, "moving training sets there." We started that mid-August and concluded in September, and we have one more unit in the hopper for deployment."

As well as her straight military duties, Gladney is involved with the SHARP program and is a Victim Advocate. She is also a master resiliency trainer. "I'm studying to be a crisis care manager, a Christian counseling program" during off-duty, she said.

Gladney wants to give credit where credit is due.

"It is not about me, it is about the Soldier," she said. "Without the Soldiers supporting me, I could do nothing. They make me look good. I give them the credit for helping me make it this far. I also give God the glory for my promotion."

☰ douglas county Sentinel

Lithia Springs family still breaking Barriers in Georgia Naional Guard

Perry first black female CW4, 21 years After father became first black colonel

By Rashad Milligan Staff Writer Sep 3, 2017

Photo illustration by Rashad Milligan/Douglas County Sentinel - Chief Warrant Four Nathanette Perry (pictured bottom left) of Lithia Springs recently became the first black woman Chief Warrant Officer Four and the first Chief Warrant Officer in the field of Information Technology in the history of the Georgia National Guard. In 1996, her father Levi H Perry became the first black Colonel in the history of the Georgia National Guard. Pictured right is Levi's article in the Sentinel when the announcement of his promotion was made. Nathanette's mother, Magnolia L. Perry, served as a lieutenant colonel in the nurse corps.

Lithia Springs resident and Chief Warrant Four Officer Nathanette Perry answered her father's challenge 21 years ago, Col. Levi H. Perry became the first black colonel in the Georgia National Guard in 1996. At a gathering to celebrate his promotion, Levi said he challenged the guard to open more doors to qualified minority officers. Now, Nathanette is breaking down more of those doors.

"I can see those challenge that I made to minority offices as well as to the military are taking place," Levi said. "I can see the light. I can see the light, you know, looking at my daughter. The first African-American woman CW4 in the Georgia Army National Guard."

Nathanette's mother, Magnolia L. Perry, also served as a lieutenant colonel in the nurse corps. Magnolia is also humbled by her daughter's accomplishment.

"Just unspeakably proud of the accomplishments she's made. Knowing that this day in age as difficult as we had it to achieve our rank and our positions, to see her do this is just outstanding," Magnolia said.

Nathanette is also the first women Chief Warrant Officer in the history of the Georgia Army National Guard.

"It signifies the importance of staying focused, believing in yourself, and dedication to service," Nathanette said. "With my parents and all they've been able to accomplish while they were in the military, it means a lot to me."

Nathanette is one of four children. The family lived in California, Virginia, and Tennessee before settling in Lithia Springs in the early 1980s. She said that watching her parents' hard work growing up inspired her along her journey. The toughest part of her military career was early on when she became a single parent. She said her support system got her through that difficult period after deployment.

Levi is still putting up challenges as he now wants her daughter to go to the highest possible rand in the Chief Warrant Officer Division, which is CW5. While he remains proud and hopes Nathanette continues her hard work, he did admit that he's worried about one issue. He doesn't want his daughter to experience Post Traumatic Stress Disorder.

"It's definitely a concern because she spent a year in Afghanistan. With us being experienced warriors ourselves, we know what can happen along the way and later on in life and all the way down the line," Levi said.

Nathanette is a graduate of Lithia Springs High School. She echoed the statements her father made 21 years ago that promotions are available to anyone who wants to accept greater responsibility.

"As long as you put in the hard work, willing to take the challenges that come with hard work. That's the main thing, that it is available to anybody," Nathanette said.

United States Army Divers Association
Meet Master Diver and former president of the U.S. Army Divers Association, Chief Warrant Officer 3 Julius Green

Mr. Green was the second African-American deepsea diver in the U.S. military and the first in the United States Army. His story is one of a young man determined to make something of himself and grateful for the chance the Army offered him for advancement in Post-World War II America. Those who know him best will tell you his is a story of dedication to the advancement of others, black, white, male and female. Many army divers owe their careers to the foresight and support they received from this incredible individual.

WOMEN'S HISTORY MONTH

Honoring and Celebrating Local Heroes
in the
Arkansas Army and Air National Guard
March 2016

Chief Warrant Officer Five Pamela Huff

Pamela (Marshall) Huff began her military career in 1975 with the Arkansas Army National Guard after graduating high school. Pamela's motivation for joining the military was in knowing that she would be serving not only her country but the people. She became the first African-American female Chief Warrant Officer Five (CW5) in the Arkansas Army National Guard (AR ARNG). Chief Huff holds the status of a Human Resource Officer & Internal Auditor for the National Guard. She earned her BS degree at John Brown University and her Master of Arts in Human Resources Development from Webster.

Adjutant General of the Arkansas National Guard shared Arkansas National Guard's photo.
· June 4, 2017 ·

It was an honor to preside over CW5 Pamela Huff's Retirement Ceremony recognizing over 41 incredible years of service to our state and nation. During the ceremony, I recognized and thanked not only Chief Huff, but her family as well, for the unwavering commitment and dedication they have given over all of these years. What a special day! Best wishes in your future endeavors Chief! #ArkansasProud!!!

CW5 Pamela Huff

Sharon Mullens, Chief Warrant Officer Four
· July 14, 2016 ·

Newly minted CW4 Sharon Mullens, AR Cyber Command, was promoted yesterday and pinned by Major General Frost, commander of US Cyber Command. CCWO Smith joined in the festivities, wishing her the best in her future with the U.S. Army Reserve.

African American Warrant Officers
Who Became Authors

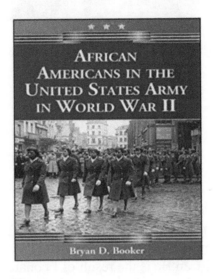

African Americans in the United States in World
War II (March 2012)
By Bryron D. Booker

The political, economic and social landscapes of the United States in the early 1940s were split by one overriding factor--race. This book explores the ways this separation extended to the military forces and the impact segregation had on World War II. Beginning with an overview of African Americans and the military from the inception of the United States and a brief history of the African American role in World War I, the focus moves to between-the-wars movements such as the Protective Mobilization Plan promoting racial integration of the military. The main focus is the African American role in World War II and the stigma that remained despite their valor. Groups discussed include the Women's Army Corps; tank destroyers; separate infantry regiments such as the 24th, 65th, 364th, 366th and 372nd; and the 2nd cavalry. Also included is a list of African American World War II veterans belatedly (and mostly posthumously) awarded Medals of Honor on January 13, 1997.

The Best Man I Can Be (November 2014)
by Leonard Dungey

    The Best Man I Can Be is the result of Leonard Dungey's 94 years of experiences. It has been written at the urging of family and friends, and a gut instinct on the part of the author to catalogue his experiences in the military as an African American and as the best man he can be. How does one become the best man he can be? Leonard Dungey strives to illustrate this through his own experiences—good and bad, local and abroad. His is a story to be remembered.

Rucksack to Brief Case: A civilian-side, job hunting guide for service members & their families! (March 2014)
By Dylan E. Raymond

"Deploying back home can be every bit as challenging as a foreign deployment....if you don't have the right training!" "With the army cutting brigades at a dozen bases around the country as well as cuts across the entire military, this information is vital!" Rucksack to Briefcase: a civilian-side job-hunting guide for service members and their families. As a veteran returning from a tour in Iraq, I was faced with the challenge of transition back to the civilian work force. Like many veterans, I learned it can be difficult whether you've served six months, two years, or an entire career in the military. There was not a single, simple guide that gave me the tools necessary to make it a smooth transition to obtain civilian employment. So, after achieving success myself, I created this short guide to address the unique challenges service members face when going from rucksack to briefcase. It includes insights, information and ideas for Creating the perfect resume Networking to get working Interviewing for success Going beyond employment and much more! Chief Warrant Officer Raymond www.civilianside.com

Camouflaged Sisters: Silent No More! (November 2016)
By Lila Holley

We see their strong, determined faces in uniform. We see their unceasing exhibition of honor and courage while protecting our country. But there is something we don't see: victims of the system—the system with the mission to protect all people of America, including its servicemembers.

In *Camouflaged Sisters: Silent No More*, twelve women strip away all comfort and protection to share the struggles they've faced, not on the battlefield, but instead in places they never expected—in their homes, in their barracks, amongst friends. These are the stories of sexual trauma, domestic violence, depression, post-traumatic stress disorder, and many other dangerous challenges women in the military fight every day.

This book gives a voice to the warrior who has suffered in silence, the soldier who has been plagued by pain, and the woman who will no longer stand for injustice but will rise up as a victor and speak her truth.

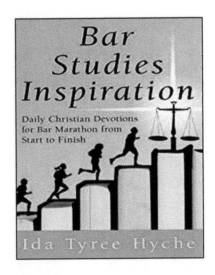

Bar Studies Inspiration – Daily Christian Devotions For Bar Marathon from Start to Finish (May 2013)
By Ida Tyree Hyche

Many professions have robust exams. But taking the Bar Exam seems to be one of the most stressful times in a person's life, occasionally causing physical ailment or emotional breakdown. Our relationship with God can carry us through hectic, nerve-wracking circumstances. We merely have to ask, believe, and receive. This book is a daily motivational devotion for Bar Exam study. Begin your Bar study marathon with day one of your study session, and end on day two or three of your Bar Exam as you finish your final lap. I trust this book will provide three to five minutes of quiet time with God per day, to calm and refresh your heart and mind with the strength to endure your Bar study marathon.

**Army Strong Women: Building the Next Generation
(January 2010)
By Melissa Leigh Farmer**

Army Strong Women represents the untold stories of the countless women who have served our country in a military position. The book represents a factual overview of military structure and history, focusing particularly on women's roles and contributions, followed by a more personalized look at individual women's experiences. Their stories tell of the struggles they overcame and the opportunities and successes they were granted by serving the Army. As a soldier herself, Melissa Farmer understands the challenges and prejudices faced by women undertaking a military career, and she offers both encouragement and practical advice to young women pursuing this vocation. Honest and informative, this book is sure to motivate and inspire all who read it.

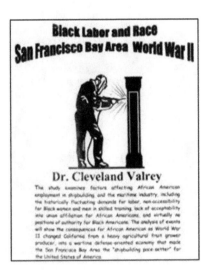

**Black Labor and Race San Francisco Bay Area World War II
(February 2004)**
By Dr. Cleveland Valrey

BLACK LABOR AND RACE "San Francisco Bay Area in World War II"; Author, Dr. Cleveland Valrey. The impact of war on African Americans has been widely debated in the American press, the mass media, and in public opinion. Did World War II represent a period of unprecedented racial progress, or did America by its unequal treatment of black people socially, in the workplace, and economically in the United States; fail to honor its stated ideals of "making the world safe for Democracy"? President Franklin Delano Roosevelt (FDR), in an address assailing Nazi propaganda relevant to human problems and actual social conditions asserted that: "The essence of our struggle today is that man shall be free. Free to live, work, worship, and pursue his own goals. There can be no real freedom for the common man without enlightened social policies. In the last analysis, they are the stakes for which the democracies are today fighting." Indeed, did the United States follow through on FDR's assertion of freedom? Is there an issue of Black Labor and Race today? Are we in new era of race and labor relations?

219

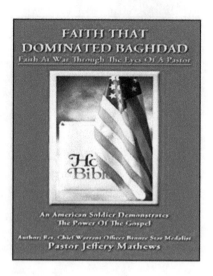

Faith That Dominated Bagdad – Faith at War Through the Eyes of a Pastor (July 2010)
By Pastor Jeffery Mathews

Faith That Dominated Baghdad is true story of an American soldier, Chief Warrant Officer and Pastor who would not allow the circumstances of war dictate who God has called him to be. This book is about understanding the power of faith and that if you learn to live by faith that you can dominate every storm in your life no matter the size of the giant. The bloody war of Baghdad Iraq was a huge giant that stood before my purpose and would bring major storms my way to cut off my destiny to cause me to give in and quit. In this book you will find out how faith when it is in its upright position can tear downs walls of intimidation, fear, and hardship and guide you to the direction that you desire to go when you walk in faith and say only what the word of God says. I discovered by living by faith while major attacks are going on in your life and even at war how you can through the words out of your mouth bring you the results that can only come when you believe what you say to come to pass. There are many that hear the gospel preached on Sunday mornings that are not getting the results that they deserve being a child of the most high God and consider themselves a Christian. What we will discover as I witnessed while serving my country and preaching the gospel with power at Baghdad Iraq bringing souls to Christ under heavy fire attacks, that the gospel cannot profit you when it is not mixed with faith. Witness the power of faith as it shuts down an enemy rocket that lands in my sleeping quarters but falls short because faith was in the house.

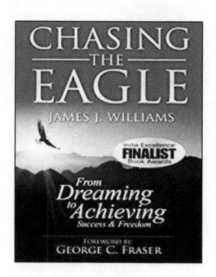

Chasing the Eagle – From Dreaming to Achieving and Freedom (April 2012)
By James J. Williams

Chasing The Eagle: From Dreaming To Achieving Success & Freedom takes away all excuses from anyone who doesn't believe they can achieve both success and financial freedom. James Williams is a man who is not sharing ideas he has read about, but rather is sharing time tested strategies he has lived! I recommend you read this book and then re-read it. It will inspire you, empower you and impact you so that you will be able to live life at the next level! Read this book...you will be glad you did!" WILLIE JOLLEY

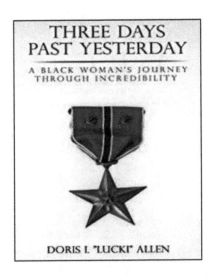

Three Days Past Yesterday: A Black Woman's Journey Through Incredibility (November 2014)
By Doris I. "Lucki" Allen

Although one might think that all the military tales of U.S. soldiers in Vietnam have been told, "Three Days Past Yesterday: A Black Woman's Journey Through Incredibility" proves that there is more to tell. Using poetry and prose, Doris I. "Lucki" Allen reveals the untold story of a black woman soldier in Vietnam. She served in military intelligence, fighting for the respect of her male peers while supplying information that could save their lives. "Three Days Past Yesterday" is not only a military tale. It is an American tale as the author paints pictures of America and of the sensibilities that she took with her to Vietnam, which include her Southern roots and experiences in a segregated America. She lets us know that the legacy of Vietnam lives on, as she and many others continue to live with PTSD and other invisible wounds of war. "Three Days Past Yesterday is a story of hope, told with the raw realities in plain sight." Bishop Yvette A. Flunder Presiding Bishop of Refuge Ministries

AS BIG As It Gets: A Chairman of the Board's Rise and Tenure at the Top – Lessons in Leadership (July 2010)
By Farrell J. Chiles

In As BIG As It Gets, Farrell J. Chiles chronicles his tenure as the Board Chair of Blacks In Government (BIG), the leading international organization for African-American public service employees. He presents his experiences, observations, and insight into leading BIG during an unprecedented period of growth. The story begins with his election on the Board of Directors and follows his journey to his election as the Chairman of the Board for five consecutive terms.

African American Warrant Officers...In Service to Our Country (January 2015)
By Farrell J. Chiles

African American Warrant Officers...In Service to Our Country tells the stories of unsung African American warrant officers who have served our country in and out of the military. This collection of historical articles, inspiring biographies, and profiles highlights the significant contributions of individual African American warrant officers from World War II to the present, with remarkable detail and language befitting their valor.

Obituaries

Chief Warrant Officer Two Justin Levon Ashley

Justin Levon Ashley of Little Rock, Ark., graduated from Jacksonville High School in 2004 and went on to further his education at Pulaski Tech receiving an Associate's Degree in Arts. He completed flight training with Central Flying Service in May 2012 obtaining his Fixed Wing License. Justin joined the Army National Guard as a PFC in 2012, as a UH60 Helicopter Repairer, where he conducted training in Ft. Eustis, Virginia. In 2014, he attended initial Rotary Wing Training at Ft. Rucker, Ala. and became a UH60 Blackhawk Helicopter Pilot. He returned to North Little Rock, AR, where he was an Aviator for B6 2-285 Aviation Regiment (Assault).

He leaves to cherish his memories: wife, Crystal; two children, Syandene and Davis; parents, Preston and Nina Ashley, LR; three sisters, Leronda (Frank) Paige, LR, Angela (Christopher) Moten, Houston, Texas, and Karin (Gerald), Sherwood, Ark.; a sister-in-law, Ann, Jacksonville, Fla.; two brothers, Preston Jr., Jacksonville, Fla. and Christopher, NLR, Ark.; three aunts, Sharon McGary, Wanda

Dorsey and Shelia Grind; one great-aunt, Geneva Williams; 10 nieces and nephews and a host of other relatives and friends.

James Delaney
April 29, 1926 - October 31, 2014
Born in Columbia, SC
Resided in Seaside, CA

James Delaney (Jim), 88 of Seaside CA passed away on Friday, October 31, 2014 surrounded by his loving family. He was born on April 29, 1926 in Columbia SC.

James was married to his adoring wife of 63 years Grace M. Delaney. They were married on June 19, 1952 at Bethlehem Baptist Church in Lawton Oklahoma.

As a child growing up in Columbia SC, he had a couple of great passions – cars and flying. He often talked about sitting for hours watching Packard Cars roll off the assembly line near his home and he was so fascinated with flying he would draw airplanes on his homework assignments.

He joined the US Army in 1944. His love of flying caused him to aspire to become an Aviator. He fulfilled his dream when he successfully completed the Warrant Officer Aviation course - becoming the first African American helicopter pilot in the US Army. In his early aviation career, he was a member of the 8th Transportation Battalion at Fort Bragg, NC. He flew single and double rotor helicopters as well as fixed wing aircraft. During the war, he evacuated the wounded, transported men and equipment to and from battle areas and laid communication lines along treetops. During one of his routine missions during the Vietnam War he was shot down and managed to escape and evade until he was picked up unharmed by friendly forces. James and his family lived all over the world, including Columbia SC, Jersey City NJ, Fort Bragg North Carolina, Fort Sill Oklahoma, Lawton Oklahoma, Fort Belvoir Virginia, Hanau Germany, Fort Devens, MA, Illesheim Germany, Fort Ord California, Seaside, California.

He was a true hero and inspired countless people with his words of encouragement and wisdom.

He was the recipient of many military awards, medals and recognition: NDSM w/10LC (National Defense Service Medal), EAME (European African-Middle Eastern Campaign Medal), Phil Lib (Philippine Liberation Ribbon) ACM (Army Commendation Medal), WWII Victory Medal, APCM (Asiatic – Pacific Campaign Medal), OAM(Japan), GCM w/2Clasps (Good Conduct Medal), UNSM (United Nations Service Medal), KSM (Korean Service Medal), ROKPUC (Republic of Korea Presidential Unit Citation), Amer Pres Unit Cit, Army Aviator Badge, AFEM (Armed Forces Expeditionary Medal), AFRM (Armed Forces Reserved Medal), Sr Army Aviator Badge, AM w/160LC (Air Medal), BSM (Bronze Star Medal), VSM (Vietnam Service Medal), RVNCM w/60dev (Republic of Vietnam Campaign Medal) and Meritorious Service Medal.

His Military education included: OCS - Officers Candidate School, Army Aviation School and Aviation Safety Course. After an esteemed career, he retired from the Army in September of 1974 as a Chief Warrant Officer 4 (CW4) after serving 30 years. He achieved the highest Warrant Officer rank at that time. He then went to work at Macy's Department store in Monterey CA as a Security Officer for 24 years.

In 1978, he received his AA degree from Monterey Peninsula College.

James was a devoted family man and had numerous hobbies and interests. He loved new technology and was an electronics aficionado.

A couple of his favorite things to do were take trips to Fry's Electronics in San Jose and attend the yearly CES (Consumer Electronics Show) in Las Vegas. He relished spending time with his family and enjoyed outings with them to attend Air shows and Air Races. He loved going to car shows with his buddy, his great-grandson Christopher Brinson. They attended the Concours d' Elegance auction and car displays together.

He was a science fiction buff - one of his favorite shows was "Dr. Who". He had a video collection that contained thousands of DVD's. He was a Photographer and owned 17 cameras at one time. He collected Coins and Stamps.

James is survived by his wife Grace Delaney of Seaside CA; Sons: James Delaney (Mitra) of Holland MI and Michael Delaney of Seaside CA; Daughters: Sheryl Delaney (Jonathan) of Yorba Linda CA, Patricia Rene Delaney-Kidd (Daniel) of Salinas CA and Stacey Delaney-Frye of Seaside CA; Sister: Lillian Edney of Columbia SC; Brother: Richard Delaney of Phoenix AZ; Grandchildren: Tiffani Delaney, Spencer Delaney, Alexander Delaney, Scott Delaney, Airianna Delaney, Julian Delaney, Kevin Delaney, Quianna Santos, Alana Delaney, Nicole Delaney, Kamiko Young, Antonio(Tony) Aaron, Jamal(JJ) Dixon, Dominic Porter, Chavon Scott, and a host of Great-Grandchildren, Nieces, Nephews, Cousins and other family and friends in various States. James is preceded in death by his son Kevin Wayne Delaney and his mother Essie Delaney.

Gilmon D. Brooks
June 24, 1925 – June 19, 2017

Gilmon was born Warren Gilmon Talbert on June 24, 1925 in Madison, WI to parents, Madeline"Madge" Mosley and Philip Talbert. At the age of 3, his parents died within months of each other. Gilmon was taken in by relatives when he arrived in Ft. Huachuca in Tombstone, AZ.

Gilmon lived through the Depression where only the basic needs were met by family and relatives. As a teen he attended Tombstone High school in 1941, and then enrolled in UCLA. During his Junior year he was approached by a US Marine recruiter to become part of the first all Black Unit formed to serve in WWII.

He enlisted in October 1943 and traveled to Montford Point Marine Base, Jackson, NC. He completed boot camp which was described as "six weeks of pure Hell!!" He graduated as an honor Man of his platoon, promoted to Private 1st Class, and became an expert Marksman. He was wounded in the battle of Iwo Jima, received a Purple Heart, Bronze star for bravery and a National Service medal and was promoted. Of the 250 Marines that went to combat, only 27 marines survived.

He returned to duty in Europe and attained the rank of Chief Warrant Officer III in the US Army in 1953. He married the former Wealthy T. Cody in Orleans, France. From That union, a son was born, Jeffrey K. Brooks. Upon retirement from military service he received a 5th Army commendation Medal to round out his career. He initially became a Manager Trainee with Sears. Gilmon returned to Federal Service as a Personnel manager with Naval weapons Station Earle, and later selected to be a Civilian Personnel manager with US Army CECOM Fort Monmouth in 1974.

After retiring from Federal Service he was actively involved in activities in Neptune Township such as, Monmouth County and NJ School Boards, Drug Board, Scouting, Monmouth County Men's Club, St. Augustine's Episcopal Church, Military Retirees Council, and The Montford Point Marines Association, Philadelphia Chapter. He is a recipient of The US Congressional Medal of Honor numerous civic awards and accommodations.

We will remember him for his love of Fine Dining, Elegant style of dress, Smooth and graceful Dancer (Once upon a time), Love of the game of Golf, Tennis, and an avid Bridge player and World traveler.

Surviving family members are his wife, Viola R. Brooks; son, Jeffrey K. Brooks (Toni) of North Brunswick, NJ; 2 grandchildren, Zachary D. Brooks and Marlo S. Brooks; former daughter-in-law, Judith Sandlin of Piscataway, NJ; 2 stepsons, Harold R. Shomo (Lenyse) of the US Virgin Islands and William J. Shomo (Janice) of Atlanta, GA; niece, Deborah Walden-Hoes; great niece, Curtistine Walden-Hoes from Northern CA area; and a host of close family, and friends that we consider family.

Retired Chief Warrant Officer - 4 James Clarence Jones
(May 12, 1933 - April 5, 2013)

Funeral: Friday April 12, 2013 at 11:00 am at Gamble Funeral Home with the Bro. Dee Newsom officiating.

Visitation: Friday April 12, 2013 at Gamble Funeral Home from 9 -11am.

Burial: Kentucky Veterans West

Clarence was born to the late Marshall Harrison Jones & Maggie Williams Jones.

He received his Master's Degree of Education from the University of Memphis. He also attended TSU where he pledged Alpha Phi Alpha Fraternity. He retired in 1995 from the Byrns Darden Elementary School.

He served in the U. S. Army for 25 yrs. retiring as a CWO4.

Clarence died April 5, 2013 in Madisonville, KY at Baptist Health Hospital.

Survivors: Wife: Carrie Brodie Jones

Mother-in-law: Clara McReynolds Brodie

Daughter: Denise Sanderson

Step - Daughter: Teresa (Austin) Moss

Sons: Derrick Jones, Darryll (Karla) Jones, David (Jessie) Jones, Stanley (Gina) Jones.

Sisters: Theodora (Walter) Harrison, Helen (Richard) Anderson & Allean Awkard

16 grandchildren, 4 great grandchildren, 6 step grandchildren, 8 step great grandchildren

Obituary of Lamont Williams

Lamont Otis Williams, Sr., age 38, of Fayetteville, NC, transitioned on Tuesday, August 22, 2017 in Fredricksburg, VA. Chief Warrant Officer Williams was born August 14, 1979 in Baltimore, MD.

On Tuesday, August 29, 2017, friends may visit Freedom Church, Vaughn C. Greene Funeral Services, 4905 York Road, Baltimore, MD 21212, from 4:00 – 8:00PM. On Wednesday, August 30, 2017, services for Chief Warrant Officer Williams will be held at St. Paul Praise and Worship Center, 501 Reisterstown Road, Pikesville, MD 21208, where the family will receive friends from 11:00 – 11:30AM with services to follow.

The interment will take place privately.

Thomas, McArthur, Jr.
Birth: Saturday, September 16, 1972
Death: Thursday, May 03, 2012 at the age of 39
Laid to Rest: Saturday, May 12, 2012 in the Chesapeake Highlands Memorial Gardens, Port Republic, Maryland

Chief Warrant Officer Four (CW4) McArthur Thomas Jr., 39, passed away on May 3, 3023 while stationed in South Korea. He was born on September 16, 1972 to the late McArthur (Mac) Thomas Sr. and Shirley (Ann) Kyler. McArthur Thomas Jr. was also known as Heavy or Mac to his family and friends.

McArthur (Heavy) attended school in the Calvert County public school system where his love for playing football and basketball started. He graduated from Calvert High School in 1990 sand started his lifelong service to defending the country he lived in by joining the United States Army in November of 1990.

McArthur started out his military career as a non-commissioned officer and later in his career advance his military status to warrant officer where he reached the grade of CW4 after 21 years of service. He served two combat tours where he was awarded and decorated for his service. McArthur graduated with a Bachelor of Business

Administration (Cum Laude) October 2007 and Master of Business Administration (Human Resource Management) May 2009 from Columbia Southern University in Florida.

McArthur leaves to cherish his son Deonte Thomas, mother Shirley (Ann) Kyler, grandmother Queenie (Ya Ya) Kyler, sister Pamela Neal (Derrick), brothers David Thomas (Tashia), Travis Smith, special friend LaKesha Griffith, nieces Tatiana and Breana Neal, nephews Jamar, Juan, Jayvell, Jervonta, and De'quan, a host of uncles, aunts, and other family and friends. McArthur has a place reserved in all of our hearts and his memory will live on forever in each of us.

Charles H. Temple
May 11, 1937 - February 20, 2017

Charles H. Temple, 79, passed away February 20, 2017. Charles was a member of Unity Missionary Baptist Church, was retired from the Camden Fairview School District and retired from the U.S. Army Reserve as a Chief Warrant Officer. Mr. Temple was preceded in death by his parents, Vincil and Mildred Temple and two sisters, Martha DeGuire and Mary Elizabeth Rock.

He is survived by his wife, Willia Mae Temple of Camden, AR; two daughters, Toni Jackson (Eli) of Conway, AR and Tia Larson (Joe) of Fredericksburg, VA; three granddaughters, Emma, Darcy, and Jasper and a sister, Leslie Toland of Clyde, TX.

ROWMELL ROARY HUGHES
May 7, 1948 - December 4, 2015

Rowmell R. Hughes, 67, of Vallejo, passed away on Friday, Dec. 4, in Martinez. She was born in Bishopville, SC.

A loving mother, grandmother, sister, aunt, and friend too many.

She is survived by one daughter; four grandchildren; two sisters, and five brothers.

She was a retired Veteran who served 38 years with the Army Reserves. She will be missed very much.

"Mom you are my hero".

Quiet hours will be held from 12 to 9 p.m., Thursday, Dec. 17, at Skyview Funeral Chapel, 200 Rollingwood Drive, Vallejo.

Homegoing service will be held on Friday, Dec. 18, at 11 a.m., at Beth Eden Baptist Church, 1183 10th St., Oakland. Burial to follow at Skyview Memorial Lawn, 200 Rollingwood Drive, Vallejo.

Conclusion

This book does not attempt to chronicle every African American Army Warrant Officer who has served. The book represents a snapshot of some outstanding Warrant Officers as an example of the many achievements and accomplishments that may have been overlooked.

From World War II to the present, African American Army Warrant Officers have served the Warrant Officer Cohort with distinction and honor. Whether a bandmaster, in Special Forces, in aviation, military intelligence, or the other branches of the military, African American Senior Warrant Officers have assumed leadership and provided mentoring and served as role models to junior Warrant Officers, enlisted, and commissioned officers.

Warrant Officers are known as "The Quiet Professionals ®". They are recognized as the "Keeper of the Keys". They are called "Chief" and officially addressed as "Mr." or "Ms." They are highly trained experts in their military occupational specialties. African American Warrant Officers are part of a proud tradition.

Their professionalism, dedication, and loyalty are beyond reproach. Outside of the military, they have served admirably in politics, the business sector, education, in civic and non-profit organizations, and other occupations.

African American Army Warrant Officers have contributed significantly to military history and American history. They have a Remarkable History.

Index

About the Author

FARRELL J. CHILES was drafted into the Army on May 26, 1970 as a private and served our country on active duty and in the Army Reserve for 38 years. He is a Vietnam Veteran and a retired Chief Warrant Officer Four. Chiles was honored as the Warrant Officer of the Year in 1998 by the United States Army Warrant Officers Association and in 1999, he was the first recipient of the Reserve Officers Association's CW4 Michael J. Novasel Outstanding Warrant Office of the Year Award. As a CW3, Chiles served on the Warrant Officer Executive Panel for the Army Leadership and Training Development Program (ATLDP). In 2016, he received the Don Hess Lifetime Achievement Award from the United States Army Warrant Officers Association.

Chiles' earlier book, "African American Warrant Officers…In Service to Our Country" won a 2015 Silver Medal Award from the Military Writers Society of America (MWSA).

Farrell Chiles resides in Phillips Ranch, California.

CPSIA information can be obtained
at www.ICGtesting.com
Printed in the USA
LVHW01*2100300518
578923LV00001B/3/P